Unless otherwise indicated, all scripture quotations are taken from the King James Version of the Bible.

a.k.a Chris Onayinka Ministries (No 6. Oweh Street, Yaba, Lagos, Nigeria.)

www.saintscommunity.net

Table of Contents

FIRST WORDS

Matthew 18:20 For where two or three are gathered together in my name, there am I in the midst of them.

Jesus speaks of a gathering of 2 or 3 gathered together in His name and He is there in the midst.

What kind of gathering is this meant to be?

Could this gathering have evolved over time with the advancement of science and technology?

Do we still retain the physical assembly of men and women who are bound by salvation through faith in Christ Jesus?

Or do we expand this narrative to either the media or different templates of human convergence?

This is the cry of this book. As we look at the Local Church in today's world.

Today's world definitely has experienced new things, scientifically, innovation-wise, that I believe was not foreseen even by writers of Scriptures.

Are we allowed to amend the intention and the message of the assembly of the saints in Christ? Either from the Old Testament books through the Four Gospels into the epistles. Are we allowed to amend them in such a way that it will suit today's fancies, fashion, and innovations? Or are we not?

This is the engagement of this book, as we trust that the believer who reads this will see through the eyes of scriptures and come to the full realization and importance of the local assembly.

We trust that as we study this together, our minds are open by the revelation found in the Lord Jesus Christ, to view, serve, appreciate, and honour the local assembly of believers.

I call you blessed!

I remain multi-dimensionally yours,

Chris Segun Onayinka

INTRODUCTION

We live in a world with its own ideas, beliefs, principles, philosophies, customs, and social behaviour. Some of these may differ from clime to clime and at times, from time to time. As we grow older and interact with the world that we live in, it is almost certain that our thought patterns or mindset, our words, actions, or reactions and eventually, our lifestyle or general outlook to life will be moulded or formed from the different things we have been exposed to from our varying backgrounds, schools, family and friends, the media and such alike.

All these put together is what eventually becomes a person's worldview. The word "worldview" is defined as the conception of the world, that is the way a person sees or views the world. A worldview is deemed as a collection of attitudes, values, stories, and expectations about the world around us which informs how we think and act. A worldview is expressed in your ethics, values, religion, philosophy, and scientific beliefs. A worldview is how a culture works out your individual practices.

So, a worldview is the way you see the world and see yourself in the world and see others in the world. It reflects in everything that you do. Your worldview is also shaped. It doesn't come from birth (that is, it is not congenital) but a concomitance of things that come through your experiences. There's no one that has a worldview from birth, it's a product of the influences that you eventually accept.

Now, for the believer in Christ, we are often faced with one of two choices, that is:

- To retain a secular or non-biblical worldview, which is often our perception of our identity and purpose in this world before salvation.

Or

- To receive and uphold a new worldview (new with respect to the unsaved man), a biblical worldview, found in the scriptures such that we begin to redefine and align our identity and purpose with what is clearly stated in God' word.

Many times, the difference between believers (and by extension, between local churches, as we will see in this book) is characterized by which of the above-mentioned worldviews they decide to have. This means that in today's world, we cannot over-emphasize the importance of having a biblical worldview whether as individual believers or as a local church. It has become quite urgent to address this wholesomely and thoroughly as we now have a growing trend of church leaders or pastors (that is, not just believers but believers charged with the responsibility of raising other believers in a local church) who have a very secular or non-biblical worldview and in some cases, they have a syncretic or syncretistic worldview where the bible is not their only source of authority in the local church but they "use" the bible alongside other secular materials (this will be further explained in the latter chapters of this book).

A Biblical worldview will be the way God sees the world and the Believer, his plans and purposes, instructions and teaching for the earth and the inhabitants and all these are contained in the books of the bible that are to be read, understood, believed and practiced by every believer and local church.

God's thought and purpose is revealed in the Scriptures, therefore as God's children our perception of ourselves or how we identify ourselves must never be from experiences, culture or societal influence but from the word of God.

> **Psalm 119:105** Thy word is a lamp unto my feet, and a light unto my path.

Thy word is the Hebrew word "dabar" which implies a word; same Greek word "logos" used by John in

> **John 1:1** In the beginning was the **Word**, and the **Word** was with God, and the **Word** was God.

The word "Logos" speaks of a person, the intent, the reason.

This person is Christ.

John 1:14 And the Word was made flesh, and dwelt among us, (and we beheld his glory, the glory as of the only begotten of the Father,) full of grace and truth. ...**Vs 29** The next day John seeth Jesus coming unto him, and saith, Behold the Lamb of God, which taketh away the sin of the world.

The word that was God in (Vs. 1) became flesh in; (Vs 14), whom John bore witness of in (Vs. 29), is Jesus "Darbar" (logos).

This same word was used in the book of Genesis.

Genesis 15:1 After these things the word of the Lord came unto Abram in a vision, saying, Fear not, Abram: I am thy shield, and thy exceeding great reward Vs 4 And, behold, the word of the Lord came unto him, saying, This shall not be thine heir; but he that shall come forth out of thine own bowels shall be thine heir. Vs 5 And he brought him forth abroad, and said, Look now toward heaven, and tell the stars, if thou be able to number them: and he said unto him, So shall thy seed be. Vs 6 And he believed in the Lord; and he counted it to him for righteousness.

Same word was used in 1st Samuel.

1st Samuel 3:1 And the child Samuel ministered unto the Lord before Eli. And the word of the Lord was precious in those days; there was no open vision. Vs 9 Therefore Eli said unto Samuel, Go, lie down: and it shall be, if he call thee, that thou shalt say, Speak, Lord; for thy servant heareth. So Samuel went and lay down in his place. Vs 10 And the Lord came, and stood, and called as at other times, Samuel, Samuel. Then Samuel answered, Speak; for thy servant heareth.

We can rightly infer from the above texts that the word of God spoken of here is a being/person.

Genesis 15:1 - The word of the Lord came to Abraham in a vision

Genesis 15:4: - The word of the Lord came unto him saying

Genesis 15:5: - He (the word of the Lord) brought him forth abroad

Genesis 15:6: - He counted it to him for righteousness

1 Samuel 3:1: - The word of the Lord was precious: there was no open vision

1 Samuel 3:1: - The Lord came and stood, and called as at other times

The person of the Lord (the word- Dabar) was present from Genesis. He was the same who spoke with Abraham and the child Samuel. The word of the Lord, the Lord Jesus Christ.

> **Revelation 1:8** I am Alpha and Omega, the beginning and the ending, saith the Lord, which is, and which was, and which is to come, the Almighty.

He is from the beginning, and he is the one, which is, and which was, and which is to come, the Lord Jesus

Back to Psalm 119:105

Thy word is a lamp unto my feet, and a light unto my path.

Christ is that light unto his (our) path.

Other references:

> **Psalm 19:8** The statutes of the LORD are right, rejoicing the heart: the commandment of the LORD is pure, enlightening the eyes.

> **Psalm 43:3** O send out thy light and thy truth: let them lead me; let them bring me unto thy holy hill, and to thy tabernacles.

> **Proverb 6:23** For the commandment is a lamp; and the law is light; and reproofs of instruction are the way of life:

> **Psalm 119:98** Thou through thy commandments hast made me wiser than mine enemies: for they are ever with me. Vs 99 I have more understanding than all my teachers: for thy testimonies are my meditation. Vs 100 I

> understand more than the ancients, because I keep thy precepts.

So, to walk in God's plan, the believer (and the local church) must have a biblical worldview.

What then is God's plan?

> **Genesis 1:27** So God created man in his own image, in the image of God created he him; male and female created he them. **Vs 28** And God blessed them, and God said unto them, Be fruitful, and multiply, and replenish the earth, and subdue it: and have dominion over the fish of the sea, and over the fowl of the air, and over every living thing that moveth upon the earth.

Notice that to be in God's image and likeness was/is to be God's representative(s). This means that to primarily understand God's plan here will be to understand man's function and to understand man's function will be to understand his identity which then defines his purpose. So, the first thing we see here is that man was/is to be God's representative in all the earth.

This task, function or responsibility is further explained in the text below.

> Genesis 2:15 And the Lord God took the man, and put him into the garden of Eden **to dress it and to keep it.**

The word "dress" was translated from the Greek word "**abad**". It implies to work, to serve, to labour. It was often used for priestly duties or service.

The word "**abad**" was applied in the following texts:

> **Genesis 2:5** And every plant of the field before it was in the earth, and every herb of the field before it grew: for the Lord God had not caused it to rain upon the earth, and there was not a man to till the ground.

> **Genesis 3:23** Therefore the Lord God sent him forth from the garden of Eden, to till the ground from whence he was taken.

The scriptures project man as the centre of activities in the earth, and all of God's plans (or workings) in the earth is woven around man. Hence, God's plans in the earth could be better understood as God's plans or workings with or through man.

This implies that God's method in the earth is man. Man is how God intends to carry out his plans in the earth and as we will see in this study, man is how God intends to reach all the nations of the earth with his message, his gospel, his kingdom.

> **Genesis 15: 13** And he said unto Abram, Know of a surety that thy seed shall be a stranger in a land that is not theirs, and shall serve them; and they shall afflict them four hundred years; **Vs 14** And also that nation,

whom they shall serve, will I judge: and afterward shall they come out with great substance

In the above text, the word serve was translated from the word "**abad**" (though here it speaks of forced service in Egypt).

Thus, the word "**abad**" is applied for service, it is rendered for a servant. It is a word largely used in Moses' writings in Exodus to Deuteronomy for the service and function of the priests in the temple.

Therefore, God's plan for man is for man to serve him. A fact that was first seen in tending to and keeping the Garden of Eden which is God's sacred place.

Exodus 3:11 And Moses said unto God, Who am I, that I should go unto Pharaoh, and that I should bring forth the children of Israel out of Egypt? Vs 12 And he said, Certainly I will be with thee; and this shall be a token unto thee, that I have sent thee: When thou hast brought forth the people out of Egypt, ye shall serve God upon this mountain.

Observe that God delivered Israel from their forced service in Egypt to bring them to the initial plan which is to serve Him and this is God's plan for humanity as a whole.

Exodus 4:22 And thou shalt say unto Pharaoh, Thus saith the Lord, Israel is my son, even my firstborn: Vs 23 And I say unto thee, Let my son go, **that he may serve** me: and if thou refuse to let him go, behold, I will slay thy son, even thy firstborn.

Israel was called out of Egypt to serve God. God saved them so they could serve and/or worship Him. Moses kept emphasizing this plan in all of his writings from Genesis through to Deuteronomy, that is, when we read either Genesis (the beginning) or subsequent books of the bible, we will come to see that man, either as an individual or as a corporate identity, was created to serve God. Man was/is to be God's priest in the earth and this was the task Adam was given.

So, in **Genesis 2:15** it is clear therefore that Moses, employed agricultural terms to explain spiritual facts (because his primary audience were agrarian). The word "abad" therefore has to do with an office, a function, a duty, or responsibility.

Thus, in **Genesis 2:15**, Moses was explaining Adam's function as God's servant or shepherd (or better still, the intended function in God's new creation).

> Genesis 2:15 And the Lord God took the man, and put him into the garden of Eden to dress it and to keep it.

The phrase "to keep" was translated from the Hebrew word "shamar".

Other references of the word shamar:

Genesis 3:24 So he drove out the man; and he placed at the east of the garden of Eden Cherubims, and a flaming sword which turned every way, to keep the way of the tree of life.

It implies to observe, to watch, to guard like a treasure, to protect or attend to.

Genesis 4:9 And the Lord said unto Cain, Where is Abel thy brother? And he said, I know not: Am I my brother's keeper?

Observe that Cain's utterance here was an aftermath of his killing of Abel. In other words, he is supposed to be his brother's keeper.

God's plan was for man to be servants (abad) of God and keeper (shamar) of his brother in the earth. Hence, God's plan was for man to be shepherds of men, but Cain did not walk in that plan.

What was God's plan for his people?

Exodus 19:6 And ye shall be unto me a kingdom of priests, and an holy nation. These are the words which thou shalt speak unto the children of Israel.

He wanted them to be a kingdom of priests in the whole earth. This was the same plan God had for Adam. Hence,

Moses in his writings unified the children of Israel that left Egypt with Adam.

Adam's role in God's new creation was to serve as a priest in God's sacred place (Garden) which in latter generations was depicted or represented by the temple or the tabernacle. The words to dress and to keep are therefore indicative of priestly duties. Thus, Moses was describing Adam's function.

Therefore, from the study above, it can be inferred that God's plan and purpose in the earth for man was to serve fellow men in a community, congregation, or an assembly that we can now refer to as the church. This is supposed to inform man's worldview. However, all through Genesis, there are patterns of a departure from God's original plan and purpose into man's individualistic, self-serving quests, often seen in the practice of idolatry, individualism. Yet, God is undeterred. He will seek out and find men in every generation to partner and work with to bring his plan to pass in the earth.

Paul reiterated that plan.

> **1st Timothy 2:3** For this is good and acceptable in the sight of God our Saviour; Vs 4 Who will have all men to be saved, and to come unto the knowledge of the truth.

His desire is to have all men saved and come to the knowledge of the truth.

What is the essence of this knowledge?

> **Ephesians 4:11** And he gave some, apostles; and some, prophets; and some, evangelists; and some, pastors and teachers; Vs 12 For the perfecting of the saints, for the work of the ministry, for the edifying of the body of Christ

From Paul's explanation in the above texts, it is evident every believer ought to be discipled (trained, nurtured, developed, equipped) in the local assembly for the work of ministry(service).

That knowledge is a training to fulfil God's plan (to serve him).

Peter opined also:

> **2nd Peter 3:9** The Lord is not slack concerning his promise, as some men count slackness; but is longsuffering to us-ward, not willing that any should perish, but that all should come to repentance.

> **Romans 10:8** But what saith it? The word is nigh thee, even in thy mouth, and in thy heart: that is, the word of faith, which we preach; Vs 9 That if thou shalt confess with thy mouth the Lord Jesus, and shalt believe in thine heart that God hath raised him from the dead, thou shalt be saved. Vs 10 For with the heart man believeth unto righteousness; and with the mouth confession is made unto salvation. Vs 11 For the

scripture saith, Whosoever believeth on him shall not be ashamed. Vs 12 For there is no difference between the Jew and the Greek: for the same Lord over all is rich unto all that call upon him. Vs 13 For whosoever shall call upon the name of the Lord shall be saved. Vs:14 How then shall they call on him in whom they have not believed? and how shall they believe in him of whom they have not heard? and how shall they hear without a preacher?

The anchor of all these questions rests on the preacher.

Until the preacher preaches, they won't hear, until they hear they won't believe, until they believe, they won't call and then be saved.

The chain of reaction leading to salvation thus is initiated by the preacher whose absence will mean no salvation.

Despite God's Omnipotence, he has made it possible to depend on a man to bring his most important desire to fruition.

The believer in Christ is the preacher. One who is available to be taught and trained via the local church so that he may be able to teach others.

Preaching is for every believer as we have all been given this ministry.

2nd Corinthians 5:17 Therefore if any man be in Christ, he is a new creature: old things are passed away; behold, all things are become new. Vs 18 And all things are of God, who hath reconciled us to himself by Jesus Christ, and hath given to us the ministry of reconciliation; Vs 19 To wit, that God was in Christ, reconciling the world unto himself, not imputing their trespasses unto them; and hath committed unto us the word of reconciliation.

Matthew 28:18 And Jesus came and spake unto them, saying, All power is given unto me in heaven and in earth. Vs 19 Go ye therefore, and teach all nations, baptizing them in the name of the Father, and of the Son, and of the Holy Ghost: Vs 20 Teaching them to observe all things whatsoever I have commanded you: and, lo, I am with you alway, even unto the end of the world. Amen.

Mark 16:15 And he said unto them, Go ye into all the world, and preach the gospel to every creature. Vs 16 He that believeth and is baptized shall be saved; but he that believeth not shall be damned

Acts 8:1 And Saul was consenting unto his death. And at that time there was a great persecution against the church which was at Jerusalem; and they were all scattered abroad throughout the regions of Judaea and Samaria, except the apostles. Vs 2 And devout men carried Stephen to his burial, and made great lamentation over him. Vs 3 As for Saul, he made havoc of the church, entering into every house, and haling men and women committed them to prison Vs 4 Therefore they that were scattered abroad went everywhere preaching the word.

Notice, those scattered abroad refer to the Church consisting of the members of the Church who went everywhere preaching the gospel. Hence, there is no other qualification needed for a believer to preach the gospel save to believe. We are saved to serve.

Philip serves as an example to every believer.

Acts 8:5 Then Philip went down to the city of Samaria, and preached Christ unto them. Vs 6 And the people with one accord gave heed unto those things which Philip spake, hearing and seeing the miracles which he did. Vs 7 For unclean spirits, crying with loud voice, came out of many that were possessed with them: and many taken with palsies, and that were lame, were healed. Vs 8 And there was great joy in that city.

This is how the local church functions in the earth. It is the responsibility of every believer.

2nd Corinthians 2:14 Now thanks be unto God, which always causeth us to triumph in Christ, and maketh manifest the savour of his knowledge by us in every place. 2:15 For we are unto God a sweet savour of Christ, in them that are saved, and in them that perish:

Moreso, Jesus referred to his disciples as the light of the world.

Matthew 5:14 Ye are the light of the world. A city that is set on an hill cannot be hid. Vs 15 Neither do men light a candle, and put it under a bushel, but on a candlestick; and it giveth light unto all that are in the house. Vs 16 Let your light so shine before men, that they may see your good works, and glorify your Father which is in heaven.

This is so as they shine the light of the glorious gospel in this dark world.

The minute you do not have this biblical worldview about the creation of man (his identity, purpose and function), it will affect how you see everything that you do and ultimately it will affect how you see the local church, its gatherings and what we do there.

Furthermore, from our earlier made explanations, we can see that at the root of disobedience and falling out of God's plan for our lives is a lack of proper recognition of our identification in Christ Jesus which should form our worldview.

Paul emphasizes this in his prayer in Philemon 6

Philemon 1:6 That the communication of thy faith may become effectual by the acknowledging of every good thing which is in you in Christ Jesus.

The word "acknowledging" was translated from the Greek word "**epignosis**" which implies: Precise, comprehension / understanding of what is ours in Christ.

The word "communication" was translated from the Greek word "Koinonia", and it implies partnership, participation, fellowship.

Therefore, Apostle Paul is saying that to the degree which the believer precisely understands every good thing which is in him, in Christ, is to the degree with which he will participate, or share in his faith.

Therefore, as believers, our realization of who we are affects everything that we do.

A believer should not define his identity by his desire or hearsay but rather see God's word as his message, purpose and plan for all men and for all ages. The subject of identity is critical to man's existence on earth and how he relates with things, people, places, and all in the earth. Thus, we have a duty to treat the Bible (God's word) very seriously. Our identity which should be obtained from the bible (which has the plan and purpose from God) can become blurred when there is a misinterpretation of its texts. This implies that when believers do not have or retain a proper biblical worldview, they begin to wander in this world without a clearly defined identity and purpose for living.

Psalm 24:1 The earth is the LORD'S, and the fullness thereof; the world, and they that dwell therein.

The Psalmist said that the earth (the place where people are) and the inhabitants of the earth belongs to God.

But Jesus in praying for his disciples in the Gospel of John begins to make distinction between the inhabitant in the earth.

John 17:9 I pray for them: I pray not for the world, but for them which thou hast given me; for they are thine. Vs:10 And all mine are thine, and thine are mine; and I am glorified in them. ...Vs:15 I pray not that thou shouldest take them out of the world, but that thou shouldest keep them from the evil. Vs:16 They are not of the world, even as I am not of the world.

The word "world" was translated from the Greek word "**Kosmos**". It refers to the earth space or its inhabitants; hence it depends on the context of the usage. It could be applied for people or earth space.

Let's also observe the way Paul used the word "kosmos".

Ephesians 2:2 Wherein in time past ye walked according to the course of this world, according to the prince of the power of the air, the spirit that now worketh in the children of disobedience: **Vs 3** Among whom also we all had our conversation in times past in the lusts of our flesh, fulfilling the desires of the flesh

> and of the mind; and were by nature the children of wrath, even as others.

The word "course" is from the Greek word "**aion**" which refers to time, activities, age, or behavioural pattern of men.

Paul used the same word as "world" in his Epistles.

> Romans 12:2 And be not conformed to this world: but be ye transformed by the renewing of your mind, that ye may prove what is that good, and acceptable, and perfect, will of God.

The word "world" applied in this instance was translated from the Greek word "**aion**" which refers to time, activities, age, or behavioural pattern of men.

Back to Ephesians 2:2

The word "world" was translated from the Greek word "**Kosmos**". Same word applied by Jesus in the **John 17** which refers to the earth space or its inhabitants.

In context of Paul's explanation, he was referring to the activities or life style of people which he said is: according to the prince of the power of the air, the spirit that now worketh in the children of disobedience.

This is not the believer. The believer by obedience to the Gospel is indwelt by the spirit of God.

Ephesians 1:13 In whom ye also trusted, after that ye heard the word of truth, the gospel of your salvation: in whom also after that ye believed, ye were sealed with that holy Spirit of promise,

He has been identified or sealed with the spirit of God.

1st Corinthians 6:17 But he that is joined unto the Lord is one spirit. **...Vs 19** What? know ye not that your body is the temple of the Holy Ghost which is in you, which ye have of God, and ye are not your own? **Vs 20** For ye are bought with a price: therefore glorify God in your body, and in your spirit, which are God's.

Therefore, by believing the Gospel of Christ one has identified with God and is not of this world. Hence, one's influence and practice should not be dictated by the behavioural pattern of this world, but by the word of God.

The believer's worldview begins from the point of faith in God. It is very critical in our worldview as believers to see that God owns everything. The earth and its inhabitants belong to God.

The believer's appraisal and appreciation of the scriptures is what determines his success in fulfilling God's plan for his life. Also, the believer's appreciation and appraisal of the truth of God's word will inform not only his worship of God, it will also inform his thinking, lifestyle and entire worldview. Therefore, being diligent with the scripture is not an option for the believer. Hence bible study demands diligence and hard work. A believer must be diligent with the Scriptures; otherwise, this can result into erroneous doctrines, beliefs and practices.

The believer must have and live by the biblical worldview. Recall, a biblical worldview is how God's word sees or views the world. This means that a believer should see the world the way God's word sees it.

Hence, once a man subscribes to faith in God (which is faith in the Gospel of Christ), it must affect his or her worldview and this implies that our worldview (as believers) must be biblical and that can only happen when the bible is properly interpreted and understood.

Thus, in our appraisal of this subject of the Church and the local church, our study and view must be according to a proper bible interpretation and not yielding to modernism (or what is today referred to as the 'new normal') to interpret scriptural truth.

If one disregards the above, then it would lead to a wrong interpretation (and application of bible truths) which would eventually affect the conduct of the believer and cause him to arrive at the wrong conclusion about God and his Word. This is because, whenever a scriptural text is misunderstood, the truth communicated by the author would be lost (on the reader). In other words, a misinterpretation of texts of scripture will affect the believer's worldview.

Therefore, the proper understanding of the terms Church and the Local church must be gotten and defined solely from the scriptures.

It is worthy of note that the writers of the Scriptures (Genesis - Malachi) read into one another. Their materials (writings) were available to be read by several generations/ audiences after them.

For instance,

> **Daniel 9:1** In the first year of Darius the son of Ahasuerus, of the seed of the Medes, which was made king over the realm of the Chaldeans; Vs 2 In the first year of his reign I Daniel understood by books the number of the years, whereof the word of the LORD came to Jeremiah the prophet, that he would accomplish seventy years in the desolations of Jerusalem.

Daniel read and taught from the writings of the prophet Jeremiah.

In Vs 2, Daniel

"...understood by books the number of the years, whereof the word of the LORD came to Jeremiah the prophet..."

There were also other writers (prophets) who read into and taught from one another.

Take for instance, if we compare/ examine the first five books attributed/credited to Moses. It can be said that what was available while they wrote were books which preceded them (the subsequent writers). Also, since Moses is attributed as the beginning of the writings (concerning God's covenant) in the Holy Scriptures, it can be said that all other writers after him, wrote and taught from His writings.

Subsequently, every other writer taught their audience from his explanation in His writings (Genesis, Exodus, Leviticus, Numbers and Deuteronomy).

In essence, every other writer taught from Moses' explanations in their (subsequent) books.

Furthermore, this implies that Moses' vocabulary (His expressions) in his writings would form a pattern of how the other writers wrote and taught in the Holy Scriptures. That is, every other prophet (in the Scriptures) picked their vocabulary (expressions) from Moses' writings. In other words, in the background of all the writings of the prophets (of God) in the Scriptures (from Joshua to Malachi) are the writings of Moses (from Genesis to Deuteronomy).

Thus, as earlier stated, the background of the entire Scriptures are the first five books of Moses (Genesis, Exodus, Leviticus, Numbers and Deuteronomy), whilst the background of the writings of Moses is the book of Genesis.

Also, it would be discovered as we study that the reason for the book of Genesis is the Exodus.

In essence, Moses' writings (explanation of God's promise- His Covenant with Abraham (Isaac and Jacob)) will be seen in all the writings of the prophets in the Scriptures. Similarly, the other prophets also taught from one another. They all read into each other. That is, for instance, Joshua obviously taught ONLY from Moses; David taught from Moses and Joshua; Isaiah taught from Moses, Joshua and David; Jeremiah taught from Moses, Joshua, David and Isaiah; Nehemiah taught from Moses, Joshua, David, Isaiah, Jeremiah and several other prophets.

It therefore suffices to say that, in the reading of the Scriptures (Genesis to Malachi), to accurately interpret texts or the intent of the authors, it is vital to understand that texts of Scriptures are relational in nature and are not to be isolated from one another. Hence, it is pertinent for the reader or Bible student/teacher in today's world to read across texts or read the entire Scriptures together as a single book (a singular document).

In today's parlance, this style of reading is similar to the community reading of the scriptures. Clearly, the New Testament writings followed the same pattern. Thus, Jesus and His Apostles in the Synoptic accounts and their Epistles all taught their respective audiences from the writings of Moses and all the prophets, in the Scriptures.

Hence, our understanding of the local church and today's world must be from the teachings of Moses and the prophets in the Scriptures, then, the Four Gospels, book of Acts and the explanation of the Apostles in the epistles. We are to uphold the never-changing truth (yet well explained and taught) of God's word in an ever-changing world.

Therefore, in this study, as we examine the local church in today's world, we will be taking our definitions and explanations from the scriptures about what the church is, what the local church is and what it is not, the role of the local church and the activities therein as well as a clear explanation on how the local church is to interact with the world today. This study will guide and help members (as well as leaders) of the local church to know who they are and what they should be doing or not do even as they relate with this present world.

CHAPTER 1

WHAT IS THE CHURCH?

In today's world, the word church is often associated with a building but as explained in the introduction of this book, it is vital for the believer to have a biblical worldview concerning people, places, events and things in the earth today. It is in that light, that we will examine what the church is in this chapter in order to have the right worldview concerning the church and the events, happenings and people therein.

The contextual application of the word church as used by the Lord Jesus is first found **Matthew 16.**

> **Matthew 16:13** When Jesus came into the coasts of Caesarea Philippi, he asked his disciples saying. Whom do men say that I the Son of man am? Vs 14 And they said. Some say that thou at John the Baptist: some, Elias and others, Jeremias, or one of the prophets. Vs. 15 He saith unto them, whom say ye that I am? Vs 16 And Simon Peter answered and said, Thou art the Chest, the Son of the living God. Vs 17 And Jesus answered and

said unto him, Blessed art thou, Simon Barjona: for flesh and blood hath not revealed it unto thee, but my Father which is in heaven. Vis 18 And I say also unto thee. That thou art Peter, and upon this rock I will build my church and the gates of hell shall not prevail against it. Vs 19 And I will give unto thee the keys of the kingdom of heaven and whatsoever thou shalt bind on earth shall be bound in heaven: and whatsoever thou shalt loose on earth shall be loosed in heaven.

Jesus asked his disciples a question: who do men say that I am? They responded based on their worldview at the time with reference to similar characters in the scriptures, and more recently, John the Baptist. Then, he asked them in verse 15, their own opinion about his identity. Then Peter spoke up and responded with the facts of his identity, which confronted the belief of the day.

What was the belief of the day?

Caesarea Philippi, was a Gentile place where worship of other gods was going on. Caesarea Philippi is where Caesar was worshipped, Caesar was called Lord, son of God. This is similar to Pharaoh in Egypt. The term "son of God" had a socio-political meaning in the Greco-Roman world[1]. This understanding helps place in context Peter's response to Jesus' question about his identity and the

[1] This concept was explained in the book "This is our God volume 5, his plans, purposes and pursuits pages 539 - 545

further response of the Lord Jesus on the same subject from **Verses 18 to 22**. In a wider sense, it also explains Jesus' response to the subject of tribute in **Matthew 22:17-22.**

That said, now observe the phrase "my Church." This term is not synonymous with Christianity. For instance, in Matthew 18:

> **Matthew 18:17** And if he shall neglect to hear them, tell it unto **the church**: but if he neglect to hear the church, let him be unto thee as an heathen man and a publican.

Observe that Jesus didn't say 'my Church' rather, he said tell it to the Church. This implies the word church was not a coinage of the Lord Jesus. The word 'church' was applied in ancient Greek from the word "**ekklesia**," which was derived from two words: 'ek' and 'Kaleo'. The word 'ek' means "out" while "kaleo" means "to call." It was applied to describe governmental assemblies in ancient Greek, to refer to those duly called out by Proper officers and possessing all political power including judicial functions.

This word was also applied by Stephen to describe the children of Israel, who were delivered from the land of Egypt.

> **Acts 7:38** This is he, that was in the church in the wilderness with the angel which spake to him in the mount Sina, and with our fathers: who received the lively oracles to give unto us

Hence, it describes the congregation/assembly of the children of Israel.

The phrase "the church" in **Matthew 18** was translated from the Greek word '**sunagoge**.' It implies an assembly of people in a place. The word '**sunagoge'** was also applied to describe set apart places of worship where the Hebrew scriptures were read and expounded to the audience. The multiplied places of worship that the **sunagoge** represented were seen in their existence to be complementary to the Jewish temple. The Jews often had places of worship instead of the temple when they were in exile or outside Jerusalem where the temple was located.

From the foregoing, it is clear that the word 'ekklesia' had its origins in the secular world. It bears mentioning that the Septuagint translated 'edah' as 'sunagoge.' The word qahal on the other hand was a bit more fluid in its translation to the Greek language. In some instances, it was translated as 'ekklesia,' and in some others as 'sunagoge.'

Vitringa gives us something to think about as he makes a distinction between these two Hebrew synonyms.

Qahal, strictly speaking, denotes an entire multitude of some people united by the bonds of society and making up a republic or a certain state, while the word edah, from the nature and force of its emphasis, speaks of only any assembly and gathering of people, whether small or large.

In the same material, he says:

Sunagoge, as also edah, always signifies an assembly joined and gathered together, although bound by no strong bond; but he ekklesia [= qahal] designates some multitude which makes up a people joined together by laws and bonds, although frequently they may happen not to be assembled or are not able to be assembled.

This distinction may have resulted in why the translators opted for ekklesia over edah.

Furthermore, Jesus applied the word "ekklesia" in both ways, to refer to the gathering and people that gather. Whenever this word is applied, attention must be given to the verbiage i.e. the language of the biblical authors of the holy scriptures, as Jesus taught from them. There this usage by Jesus was to point the attention of his disciples to a specific kind of people. He was speaking of a specific people to be called out, and his audience understood this.

Another word Jesus used in his response to Peter's submission is the word 'build'. The word "build was translated from the Greek word "oikodomeo," it implies to found or build a house. It was coined from two Greek words oikos and doma. The word oikos[2] refers to a house while the word doma means to build. It can be inferred from the application of the word "build" or "built," that it refers to something built once and not an on-going work.

[2] It was used in the following texts of scripture: Matthew 7:24-26, Matthew 21:33, Matthew 23:29

Putting this in context, it thus can read" ...I will establish my called out ones...". Hence, the Church is built/established only by Jesus: He is the head even the source of the Church.

Let us have a closer observation of other phrases in that conversation.

> Matthew 16:18 And I say also unto thee, That thou art Peter, and upon this rock I will build my church; and the gates of hell shall not prevail against it.

The Gates of Hell.

This is a specific place which can be described as where they interact with the spirit world[3]. A similar phrase was used by Jacob in **Genesis 28:12-14** (gate of heaven) to refer to the place of God's interaction with man (the earth).

<u>Prevail</u>

> Matthew 16:18 And I say also unto thee. That thou art Peter, and upon this rock I will build my church; and the gates of hell shall not **prevail** against it.

The word "prevail" was translated from the Greek word **katischuo**; it implies to withstand or overpower. The word was also applied in the text below:

---

[3] Algie, B. 2016. Caesarea Philippi. In J. D. Barry, D. Bomar, D. R. Brown, R. Klippenstein, D. Mangum, C. Sinclair Wolcott, W. Widder (Eds.), The Lexham Bible Dictionary. Bellingham, WA: Lexham Press.

Luke 23:23 And they were instant with loud voices, requiring that he might be crucified. And the voices of them and of the chief priests prevailed.

This therefore shows that the 'gates of hell' shall not overpower the Church of Jesus Christ. Hence, he speaks of the authority of Jesus Christ in the church, which is over that of the gate of hell. This highlights a major worldview of the scriptures - the supernatural/spiritual worldview context of the earth. This worldview was prevalent in the Old Testament books with the highpoint being Moses and the gods of Egypt (Exodus 7 - 15). This worldview was also retained by the writers of the New Testament books; this helps explain why Jesus' next statement was about authority in **Verse 19.**

Matthew 16:19 And I will give unto thee **the keys** of the kingdom of heaven: and whatsoever thou shalt bind on earth shall be bound in heaven: and whatsoever thou shalt loose on earth shall be loosed in heaven.

The word "keys" refers to authority. Hence, the authority of the kingdom of heaven' refers to the authority of Christ in the Church, which is for God's plan for the whole earth. (Matthew 28:18-20). So, the church of Christ is established in its fulness upon the resurrection of Christ. And it is expanding as men are added to the church via the preaching of the message of God's plan for the whole earth (the gospel) - **Matthew 28:18-20, Mark 16:20, Acts 2:47.**

Recall, we explained earlier that the church refers to both the gathering and the people that gather. This concept was also explained in the epistles; they referred to the church as 'his body' - **Ephesians 1:22-23, Ephesians 4:4-5, 1st Corinthians 12:12,27, Ephesians 5:23-25.**

One can readily see the body of Christ and its constituents from the above scriptures which lends credence to the fact that the terms 'body of Christ' and 'the church' are synonymous.

There are other words used in the scriptures to refer to the church or the body of Christ.

> **Galatians 6:10** As we have therefore opportunity, let us do good unto all men especially unto them who are of the **household of faith.**

The church is referred to as the household of faith. The word "household" was translated from the original word **'oikeios'**, which implies a family. It refers to one identity.

This terminology was also explained by Paul in his letter to the Ephesians.

> **Ephesians 2:19** Now therefore ye are no more strangers and foreigners, but fellowcitizens with the saints, and of the household of God;

He refers to the church as the household of God, that is, the family of God.

> **Ephesians 3:14** For this cause I bow my knees unto the Father of our Lord Jesus Christ, Vs 15 Of whom the whole family in heaven and earth is named,

The word 'family' was translated from the Greek word **'patria'** which implies paternal descent, invariably it refers to a whole race, a nation. This nation is one, both in heaven and in the earth. This clearly shows an assembly in/of one family, a nation. God's new creation.

Again, worthy of note is the fact that Jesus' body (The Church) is always spoken of as a spiritual gathering of different nations, tribes and genders in one person.

> **Galatians 6:10** As we have therefore opportunity, let us do good unto all men especially unto them who are of the household of faith.

The word "household" was translated from the Greek word "**oikeios**"; which implies family, a set of people with the same heritage by birth, that is, a common possession. the root word "**oikos**"; which implies home, a family, or house. Hence, faith is common to this family, a common possession in this family. It was used also in **Ephesians 2:18.**

> **Ephesians 2:18** For through him we both have access by one Spirit unto the Father. Vi 19 Now therefore ye are no more strangers and foreigners, but fellow citizens with the saints, and of the household of God;

A similar word was also used in **Titus 1:4** and **Romans 1:12.**

> **Titus 1:4** To Titus, mine own son after the **common** faith: Grace, mercy, and peace, from God the Father and the Lord Jesus Christ our Saviour.

The word "common" was translated from the Greek word "**koinos**"; which implies "shared by all." Hence faith is shared by all in the household of faith.

> **Romans 1:12** That is, that I may be comforted together with you by the **mutual** faith both of you and me.

The word "mutual" implies that no member of this family lacks faith.

> **Romans 10:17** So then faith cometh by **hearing**, and **hearing** by the word of God.

The word hearing was translated from the Greek word "**akoe**"; which implies what was heard. What was heard is further explained as the word of God or the gospel of our Lord Jesus Christ.

So, the believer receives faith by the word of God, the gospel of Christ and in the same vein is Christ's called out one and part of the body of Christ (the church).

Thus, when the gospel is preached, and a man believes the gospel, he is baptized into the body of Christ. That is, he is identified in the body. He is of the household of faith.

It is therefore clear to see that the believer is not born into isolation but into a family. Furthermore, as his church is his family which is by his spirit. This implies that every member of this family is spiritual. (**1st Corinthians 2:12-14**).

The question then will be this, Is the Church of Christ an afterthought or God's intention from the beginning?

God made man a relational being. This means that God created man not to be alone but to have relationships. Everybody comes into this world via relationships (a male man and a female man); we were all born into this world by our parents, and we did not appear mysteriously into this world.

We have different kinds of relationships in the natural - Parent/Child relationships, Sibling relationships, Workplace/educational relationships et al. These relationships were made by God to help man and make him/her carry out God's will in the earth.

We see in the Scriptures that God created Adam and brought him into a relationship with the woman Eve; the two of them were given instructions concerning God's will and plan for the earth **(Genesis 1:26-30)**. The same instruction (promise and plan) was given to Abel, Enoch, Noah and other men concerning the earth as God's house, his resting place, his ever-abiding residence with man but men rejected God's plan (**Genesis 6:1-4, Genesis 11**). God re-echoed the same promise and plan to Abraham (**Genesis 12:3, Genesis 15:6**) in him shall all the nations of the earth be blessed. Isaac, Abraham's son believed in this promise same with Jacob his son who had an encounter with the Lord in **Genesis 28:12-16**. Joseph, Jacob's son likewise believed in this same promise and was able to preserve God's people (Jacob's family) in Egypt from the famine. It is important to note that all of God's dealings in the earth has been through men which explains why God would also come as a man to save man. It was never restricted to only the male man; God used and uses both the male man and the female man to accomplish his plan and purpose in the earth.

In Egypt, Jacob's family grew into a nation and while leaving Egypt they sojourned in the wilderness as an assembly or a congregation. The nation of Israel was given the same promise and plan in the beginning to be God's son, God's priest, God's prophet, God's method in all the earth.

> **Exodus 4:22** And thou shalt say unto Pharaoh, Thus saith the LORD, Israel *is* my son, *even* my firstborn:

He called them his special people:

> **Deuteronomy 7:6** For thou *art* an holy people unto the LORD thy God: the LORD thy God hath chosen thee to

be a special people unto himself, above all people that *are* upon the face of the earth.

Deuteronomy 14:2 For thou *art* an holy people unto the LORD thy God, and the LORD hath chosen thee to be a peculiar people unto himself, above all the nations that *are* upon the earth.

God wants the nation of Israel to be priests and kings in the earth.

Exodus 19:6 And ye shall be unto me a kingdom of priests, and an holy nation. These *are* the words which thou shalt speak unto the children of Israel.

Recall that man is a relational being, likewise God is a relational being and he wants man to also relate with him, however, through men.

Therefore, the nation of Israel was called out of the bondage and oppression of Egypt unto an assembly, to be God's son.

Exodus 6:6-8 Wherefore say unto the children of Israel, I *am* the LORD, and I will bring you out from under the burdens of the Egyptians, and I will rid you out of their bondage, and I will redeem you with a stretched out arm, and with great judgments: Vs 7 And I will take you to me for a people, and I will be to you a God: and ye shall know that I *am* the LORD your God, which bringeth you out from under the burdens of the

Egyptians. Vs 8 And I will bring you in unto the land, concerning the which I did swear to give it to Abraham, to Isaac, and to Jacob; and I will give it you for an heritage: I *am* the LORD.

Now, there are references to that assembly of Israel in the scriptures. Some include:

Exodus 12:3 Speak ye unto all the congregation of Israel, saying, In the tenth day of this month they shall take to them every man a lamb, according to the house of their fathers, a lamb for an house:

Exodus 12:6 And ye shall keep it up until the fourteenth day of the same month: and the whole assembly of the congregation of Israel shall kill it in the evening.

Exodus 12:43 And the LORD said unto Moses and Aaron, This *is* the ordinance of the passover: There shall no stranger eat thereof: Vs 44 But every man's servant that is bought for money, when thou hast circumcised him, then shall he eat thereof. Vs 45 A foreigner and an hired servant shall not eat thereof. Vs 46 In one house shall it be eaten; thou shalt not carry forth ought of the flesh abroad out of the house; neither shall ye break a bone thereof. Vs 47 All the congregation of Israel shall keep it.

The word "congregation" refer to that assembly.

Since Israel had that responsibility God has given to them, Moses was to make known to the people of Israel the precepts of God.

> **Exodus 18:13** And it came to pass on the morrow, that Moses sat to judge the people: and the people stood by Moses from the morning unto the evening.

> **Deuteronomy 4:4** But ye that did cleave unto the LORD your God *are* alive every one of you this day. **Vs**
> **5** Behold, I have taught you statutes and judgments, even as the LORD my God commanded me, that ye should do so in the land whither ye go to possess it. **Vs**
> **6** Keep therefore and do *them;* for this *is* your wisdom and your understanding in the sight of the nations, which shall hear all these statutes, and say, Surely this great nation *is* a wise and understanding people. Vs
> 7 For what nation *is there so* great, who *hath* God *so* nigh unto them, as the LORD our God *is* in all *things that* we call upon him *for?* Vs 8 And what nation *is there so* great, that hath statutes and judgments *so* righteous as all this law, which I set before you this day?

Moses was to teach them the statues and judgments of the Lord.

Therefore, the children of Israel were to be taught the statutes and judgment of God in the assembly, they were to walk in it and that is their love for God. So, their love for God is seen in their worship of God, how they assemble, hear God's word and act on God's word.

Deuteronomy 6:4 Hear, O Israel: The LORD our God *is* one LORD: Vs 5 And thou shalt love the LORD thy God with all thine heart, and with all thy soul, and with all thy might. Vs 6 And these words, which I command thee this day, shall be in thine heart: Vs 7 And thou shalt teach them diligently unto thy children, and shalt talk of them when thou sittest in thine house, and when thou walkest by the way, and when thou liest down, and when thou risest up. Vs 8 And thou shalt bind them for a sign upon thine hand, and they shall be as frontlets between thine eyes. Vs 9 And thou shalt write them upon the posts of thy house, and on thy gates. Vs 10 And it shall be, when the LORD thy God shall have brought thee into the land which he sware unto thy fathers, to Abraham, to Isaac, and to Jacob, to give thee great and goodly cities, which thou buildedst not,

In other words, in God's earth, God's temple, our love for God is seen in how we listen, meditate and practice his word.

Nehemiah 8:4 And Ezra the scribe stood upon a pulpit of wood, which they had made for the purpose; and beside him stood Mattithiah, and Shema, and Anaiah, and Urijah, and Hilkiah, and Maaseiah, on his right hand; and on his left hand, Pedaiah, and Mishael, and Malchiah, and Hashum, and Hashbadana, Zechariah, *and* Meshullam. Vs 5 And Ezra opened the book in the sight of all the people; (for he was above all the people;)

and when he opened it, all the people stood up: Vs 6 And Ezra blessed the LORD, the great God. And all the people answered, Amen, Amen, with lifting up their hands: and they bowed their heads, and worshipped the LORD with *their* faces to the ground. Vs 7 Also Jeshua, and Bani, and Sherebiah, Jamin, Akkub, Shabbethai, Hodijah, Maaseiah, Kelita, Azariah, Jozabad, Hanan, Pelaiah, and the Levites, caused the people to understand the law: and the people *stood* in their place. Vs 8 So they read in the book in the law of God distinctly, and gave the sense, and caused *them* to understand the reading.

Ezra, here, just like Moses took time to explain the word of the Lord to the people while they were in exile.

The practice of gatherings as worship of God continued even with Jesus in the four gospels.

Matthew 5:1-2 And seeing the multitudes, he went up into a mountain: and when he was set, his disciples came unto him: Vs 2 And he opened his mouth, and taught them, saying,

He taught the gathering that was with him. The parable of the sower (**Mark 4; Matthew 13 and Luke**) was also done in public gatherings while he taught his disciples even more privately. Jesus, upon his resurrection instructed his disciples not to leave Jerusalem.

Luke 24:49 And, behold, I send the promise of my Father upon you: but tarry ye in the city of Jerusalem, until ye be endued with power from on high.

The apostles kept on gathering as worship of God; they kept praying.

Acts 1:14 These all continued with one accord in prayer and supplication, with the women, and Mary the mother of Jesus, and with his brethren.

Hence, on the day of Pentecost, it was in one those gatherings that they spoke with tongues.

Acts 2:1 And when the day of Pentecost was fully come, they were all with one accord in one place. Vs 2 And suddenly there came a sound from heaven as of a rushing mighty wind, and it filled all the house where they were sitting. Vs 3 And there appeared unto them cloven tongues like as of fire, and it sat upon each of them. Vs 4 And they were all filled with the Holy Ghost, and began to speak with other tongues, as the Spirit gave them utterance.

The gathering stirred up evangelism as they reached out to surrounding men and women with the gospel. The apostles preached and many got saved by the gospel of Christ.

Acts 2:41 Then they that gladly received his word were baptized: and the same day there were added *unto them* about three thousand souls. Vs 42 And they continued stedfastly in the apostles' doctrine and fellowship, and in breaking of bread, and in prayers.

The people who are now believers received teaching (doctrine) from the apostles and kept gathering with them.

Paul's method of raising disciples is also that he taught them:

Acts 19:9 But when divers were hardened, and believed not, but spake evil of that way before the multitude, he departed from them, and separated the disciples, disputing daily in the school of one Tyrannus.

In Acts 20, Paul mentioned how he had meetings in small and large numbers.

Acts 20:20 *And* how I kept back nothing that was profitable *unto you,* but have shewed you, and have taught you publickly, and from house to house,

Those meetings which are patterns from the exodus is what has evolved into what we have today as the local church i.e. gatherings of believers in a particular location. The local church or what we term as Church today is **the physical gathering of the believers, in a particular location with definite leadership. It is God's house, his heaven and earth where his plan, purpose and pursuits are carried out in the earth today.**

Church meetings are so important that the epistles that were written were written majorly to the congregation or to the leaders who lead or pastor those congregations. Therefore, as believers, we are not to ignore the gathering of believers together. It is important because it is our worship of God. The writer of the book of Hebrews warns about not attending church gatherings.

> **Hebrews 10:24** And let us consider one another to provoke unto love and to good works: Vs 25 Not forsaking the assembling of ourselves together, as the manner of some *is;* but exhorting *one another:* and so much the more, as ye see the day approaching.

So, the term "**church**" has been understood in physical gathering or assembly and as an identity which we have in Christ Jesus. For instance, in Matthew 18, when Jesus said "tell it to the church":

> **Matthew 18:16** But if he will not hear *thee, then* take with thee one or two more, that in the mouth of two or three witnesses every word may be established. Vs 17 And if he shall neglect to hear them, tell *it* unto the church: but if he neglect to hear the church, let him be unto thee as an heathen man and a publican. Vs 18 Verily I say unto you, Whatsoever ye shall bind on earth shall be bound in heaven: and whatsoever ye shall loose on earth shall be loosed in heaven.

He was referring to the local assembly, the gathering of believers where you assemble on a regular basis.

The Church is a Physical Gathering

The advent of online communication and the internet of things should not make the believer neglect the instruction of gatherings. Technology improves our world today, but we should not seek to modify the instructions found in the scriptures about gatherings. Technology should always be the exception in human interaction and not the norm. God has made and reserved many things for physical contact and communication.

Jesus gave specific instructions meant for specific locations.

> **Matthew 28:16** Then the eleven disciples went away into Galilee, into a mountain where Jesus had appointed them.

Even upon the resurrection of Jesus, they still met in a physical place.

Acts 9:6 And he trembling and astonished said, Lord, what wilt thou have me to do? And the Lord said unto him, Arise, and go into the city, and it shall be told thee what thou must do.

The to-be apostle was told to go to a place. The book of revelation had instructions for churches who gathered in specific places.

> **Revelation 1:11** Saying, I am Alpha and Omega, the first and the last: and, What thou seest, write in a book, and send it unto the seven churches which are in Asia; unto Ephesus, and unto Smyrna, and unto Pergamos, and unto Thyatira, and unto Sardis, and unto Philadelphia, and unto Laodicea.

The concept of an assembly is similar to when we buy some device. It comes in parts initially, but the parts need to be fitted together or assembled for it to begin to function. The church is similar.

> **Ephesians 4:16** From whom the whole body fitly joined together and compacted by that which every joint supplieth, according to the effectual working in the measure of every part, maketh increase of the body unto the edifying of itself in love.

An assembly/physical gathering fulfils this scripture. Believers should not be found trying to review clear biblical instructions.

> **Acts 6:3** Wherefore, brethren, look ye out among you seven men of honest report, full of the Holy Ghost and wisdom, whom we may appoint over this business.

> **1 Corinthians 6:5** I speak to your shame. Is it so, that there is not a wise man among you? no, not one that shall be able to judge between his brethren?

If the church was not gathering physically, how would these instructions be carried out?

That local church should have a definite leadership and order.

> **1 Thessalonians 5:12** And we beseech you, brethren, to know them which labour among you, and are over you in the Lord, and admonish you;

But it must gather and not in anonymity.

My Role in the Church

As important as it is to attend our local churches, it is also important not to be idle there. As believers, we are expected to minister in our local assembly and to other believers. Ministry can be understood in precept and example as portrayed by Christ Jesus.

> **Matthew 20:28** Even as the Son of man came not to be ministered unto, but to minister, and to give his life a ransom for many.

The word "minister" means to serve or to wait upon. It is a word used for a deacon. Jesus referenced the word for himself to explain and describe his service to the world. That service was for him to give himself as a ransom. This was to explain the work he was to accomplish—his death, burial and resurrection.

Paul also related to Jesus' ministry;

> **Romans 15:8** Now I say that Jesus Christ was a minister of the circumcision for the truth of God, to confirm the promises made unto the fathers:

The word "minister" was also referenced for angels, that is, they wait on instructions to serve:

> **Hebrews 1:7** And of the angels he saith, Who maketh his angels spirits, and his ministers a flame of fire.
>
> **Hebrews 1:13** But to which of the angels said he at any time, Sit on my right hand, until I make thine enemies thy footstool? Vs 14 Are they not all ministering spirits, sent forth to minister for them who shall be heirs of salvation?The ministry of angels is to minister for the heir of salvation in that context was talking about the old testament, because he calls them heirs of salvation.

The word "ministering" implies to be addicted or **employed to serve**. Hence angels are to minister for man.

Now, in the book of Acts, ministry was defined by what Jesus did;

> **Acts 1:17** For he was numbered with us, and had obtained part of this ministry.

What ministry was referred to?

What Jesus committed to them in the synoptic four gospel

> **Matthew 10:1** And when he had called unto him his twelve disciples, he gave them power against unclean spirits, to cast them out, and to heal all manner of sickness and all manner of disease.

> **Luke 9:1-5** Then he called his twelve disciples together, and gave them power and authority over all devils, and to cure diseases. Vs 2 And he sent them to preach the kingdom of God, and to heal the sick. Vs 3 And he said unto them, Take nothing for your journey, neither staves, nor scrip, neither bread, neither money; neither have two coats apiece. Vs 4 And whatsoever house ye enter into, there abide, and thence depart. Vs 5 And whosoever will not receive you, when ye go out of that city, shake off the very dust from your feet for a testimony against them.

Jesus sent his disciples out to preach the gospel of the kingdom of God. This was based on the previous statement he made;

> **Matthew 9:37** Then saith he unto his disciples, The harvest truly is plenteous, but the labourers are few; vs 38 Pray ye therefore the Lord of the harvest, that he will send forth labourers into his harvest.

But prior to this, Jesus was the only one preaching,

Matthew 9:35 And Jesus went about all the cities and villages, teaching in their synagogues, and preaching the gospel of the kingdom, and healing every sickness and every disease among the people.

Matthew 4:23 And Jesus went about all Galilee, teaching in their synagogues, and preaching the gospel of the kingdom, and healing all manner of sickness and all manner of disease among the people.

So, in Acts 1:17, the ministry Peter was referring to was the preaching of the gospel.

Thus, we see ministry as the ministry of Jesus, and what he has committed to the church, through the apostles. Ministry gifts therefore will be understood as the functions/activities of Christ in his resurrection in and through the church.

In his epistles, Paul gave a clear explanation to the ministry gifts in the body of Christ.

Ephesians 4:7 But unto every one of us is given grace according to the measure of the gift of Christ. Vs 8 Wherefore he saith, When he ascended up on high, he led captivity captive, and gave gifts unto men. Vs 9 (Now that he ascended, what is it but that he also descended first into the lower parts of the earth? Vs 10 He that descended is the same also that ascended up far above all heavens, that he might fill all things.) vs 11

And he gave some, apostles; and some, prophets; and some, evangelists; and some, pastors and teachers;

Paul in explaining this referred to David's Psalms;

Psalms 68:18 Thou hast ascended on high, thou hast led captivity captive: thou hast received gifts for men; yea, for the rebellious also, that the LORD God might dwell among them.

The word '**grace'** means what is freely given for the benefit of the recipient; favour; gift; something not worked for. So, grace is seen first in the person of Jesus.

Titus 2:11 For the **grace** of God that bringeth salvation hath appeared to all men,

Ephesians 2:8 For by **grace** are ye saved through faith; and that not of yourselves: it is the gift of God:

He calls salvation the work of grace in Christ. But in **Ephesians 4:7**, the grace was in reference to ministry.

Now, the word 'gave' in Ephesians 4:8 means what is for the benefit of the recipient. Paul's reference of the terms 'given and grace' was to emphasis what Christ made available upon his resurrection. This implies that what is "given" has to be received". Hence, the giver is distinct from the receiver.

For instance;

John 1:12 But as many as received him, to them gave he power to become the sons of God, even to them that believe on his name:

Who gave the right to become sons of God?

God and this is through Christ Jesus. Who were those that received him? Those that believe on his name

Also,

Acts 2:33 Therefore being by the right hand of God exalted, and having received of the Father the promise of the Holy Ghost, he hath shed forth this, which ye now see and hear.

NB: The statement ... "Having received of the Father"

The discourse was about what was "seen and heard" (utterance) which led to the subject matter of repentance (Vs38-40).

Acts 1:5 For John truly baptized with water; but ye shall be baptized with the Holy Ghost not many days hence.

Again, Jesus is the one that baptizes with the Holy Ghost. This was gotten from John the Baptist (Matthew3:11)

Who receives of the Father (Act2:33)?

The recipients of the utterance. That was what got the attention of the audience. Therefore, this was not in reference to Jesus receiving from the Father, because he is the giver. Hence, what is given, that is, grace, is in reference to ministry (not grace for salvation).

Back to Ephesians 4:7

> **Ephesians 4:7** But unto every one of us is given grace according to the measure of the gift of Christ.

The word "measure" is to talk of the different functions or ministry gifts in the body which was eventually mentioned in verse 11.

> **Ephesians 4:11** And he gave some, apostles; and some, prophets; and some, evangelists; and some, pastors and teachers;

> **Romans 12:3** For I say, through the grace given unto me, to every man that is among you, not to think of himself more highly than he ought to think; but to think soberly, according as God hath dealt to every man the measure of faith.

Observe, the use of the word "**measure of faith**" which describes different portions.

> **Romans 12:4** For as we have many members in one body, and all members have not the same office:

The word "member" means a part of the body while the word "office" means function. He was using an illustration of the physical body to describe the function of believers how we all depend on one another.

Therefore, the gifts that God gives are the gifts available only in Christ. That which is resident in the body of Christ is a function of what Christ accomplished by his resurrection and now given. And because of this, every believer is expected to function with the gift of Christ in the local church. **A believer is expected to minister to other believers and to serve in the local assembly where he is found. He is expected to function and serve with the gifts of the spirit**.

> **1 Corinthians 12:8-10** For to one is given by the Spirit the word of wisdom; to another the word of knowledge by the same Spirit; Vs 9 To another faith by the same Spirit; to another the gifts of healing by the same Spirit; Vs 10 To another the working of miracles; to another prophecy; to another discerning of spirits; to another *divers* kinds of tongues; to another the interpretation of tongues:

> **1 Corinthians 14:26** How is it then, brethren? when ye come together, every one of you hath a psalm, hath a doctrine, hath a tongue, hath a revelation, hath an interpretation. Let all things be done unto edifying.

When we come together, we come to bless other believers by the spirit of God.

More so, a believer should also serve in the natural affairs in his local assembly. The deacons who were chosen in Acts 6 were full of the holy spirit and wisdom yet they were to serve food.

> **Acts 6:1-3** And in those days, when the number of the disciples was multiplied, there arose a murmuring of the Grecians against the Hebrews, because their widows were neglected in the daily ministration. Vs 2 Then the twelve called the multitude of the disciples *unto them,* and said, It is not reason that we should leave the word of God, and serve tables. Vs 3 Wherefore, brethren, look ye out among you seven men of honest report, full of the Holy Ghost and wisdom, whom we may appoint over this business.

This was how Philip and also Stephen were chosen. Philip later went to Samaria to preach Christ.

> **Acts 11:28-30** And there stood up one of them named Agabus, and signified by the Spirit that there should be great dearth throughout all the world: which came to pass in the days of Claudius Caesar. Vs 29 Then the disciples, every man according to his ability, determined to send relief unto the brethren which dwelt in Judaea: Vs 30 Which also they did, and sent it to the elders by the hands of Barnabas and Saul.

Here, we find Barnabas and Saul who were prophets sent on an errand by the church to send palliatives to other brethren. In the four gospels, the apostles of Jesus were the chief distributors of food when Jesus fed the multitude. This implies that while the apostles functioned and served with spiritual things, they also served with natural things.

As believers, our local assembly is requiring people to function in the natural affairs. Our local church needs us to be a blessing to other believers. It could be to arrange, clean or dust the seats, to keep the floor clean, get the sound ready or something that will help another believer. We should not be found idle in church.

Be committed to the Church

The local church refers to a gathering of believers in a particular location and is a part of the universal church, the body of Christ which consist of believers in every part of the world (Romans 12:5, 1 Corinthians 12:12, Eph 2:12).

Finding a local church, as simple as it may sound requires the wisdom of God's word and so does getting and staying committed there.

The issue will not be to locate the venue of one especially since there's almost one or two on every street nowadays.

Deciding on which local church to identify with is a serious matter and should be done PRAYERFULLY AND PURPOSEFULLY. Its closeness to your place of residence, a common consideration with many people today would be unwise, because many travel sometimes all the way abroad to study or to get medical attention, which is an indication of a desire for the best available, therefore the same attitude should be employed for something as important and eternal as locating a church to attend.

If you take your Christian life seriously, you should choose to attend the best local church around you. While it's easy to get carried away by GOOD MUSIC, SHORT MESSAGE & SERVICE (SMS) AND NICE LOOKING USHERS and FIRST TIMER GIFTS AND FOOD PACKS.

Some are even carried away by activities, they are not learning the word of God or growing up spiritually in the church they play the keyboard, play the drums, are in drama group etc.

They would rather be involved in activities than grow up spiritually. Others yet still are in a particular church because "It's our family church", "my friends are in the church" or "I have connections there".

All these considerations though may make sense to the carnal man, have no spiritual benefit.

Before you choose a local church, ask yourself these questions:

Question 1: Do I want to Grow Spiritually?

If yes, then you must choose to attend a local church where the teaching of God's word is given first place and every member is closely mentored and monitored to understand every bible doctrine.

WHY? Because spiritual growth will only come with growth in the knowledge of God's word-Jesus Christ (John 1:1-5, 9-16, 1Peter 2:2, Acts 20:20). Spiritual growth will come by the revelation of who Jesus is, all he has done for us and all we can do because we are in Him (Col. 1:9, Eph 1:19, 3:16-19, Philemon 6).

Question 2: Do I Want to Consistently See God's Divine Hand in All my Affairs in Life?

If yes! Then you must attend a local church where a lot of time is devoted to prayer and particularly praying in the spirit (in tongues)

WHY? Because prayer is a demonstration of our trust in and our dependence upon God. By prayer, great power; God's power is made available for everyone in life situations and circumstances, thus the bible teaches us to pray fervently (James 5:16) and to pray always in the spirit (Eph 6:18) praying in the spirit is praying in tongues (1 Corinthians 14:2, 4, 15, 18, Jude 20).

Question 3: Do I Want to Walk in the Will of God for my Life?

If yes again! Then you must choose a local church that Is in the will of God. And how can you tell? It must be a local church where EVANGELISM and reaching the lost is not treated with levity or taken as a pastime but, is approached with a deep sense of purpose and responsibility and is receive, as a commission of JESUS CHRIST, the head of the church (Matthew 28:18, Mark 16:15-20).

WHY? Staying in the will of God for your life starts with obeying God in general instructions and paying attention to light in His word with which comes more specific instructions (Romans 12:2).

Question 4: Do I Want to Live Far Above the Forces of Darkness of the World?

Again if Yes! Excitedly so! Then you must attend a local church where there's an atmosphere of LOVE, JOY AND FAITH IN GOD'S WORD.

WHY? Because the system of this world is ruled by the god of this world, the devil (2 Cor. 4:4, Eph 2:2).

The believer will only win in life all the time by putting on the whole armor of GOD (Eph 6:10-18) How is that Possible? 1John 5:4 a faith filled life.

Question 5: Do I Want to be a Blessing to Others and Flow with the Gifts of the Spirit?

Sure Yes! Then you must attend a local church where room is given to each one to express things of and things pertaining to the spirit, tongues, interpretations of tongues, prophecies, among other (1Cor. 14:12-15).

WHY! Because things of the spirit will only improve with practice (1Cor.12:31, 14:39, Hebrews 5:14).

Staying committed to a local church must be with the understanding that the local church is God's plan for the believer, a place where he has a pastor who teaches and trains him spiritually, who is responsible to bring to him correction, reproof, and instructions in righteousness (2 Timothy 3:16). The local church therefore has spiritual leaders who have Christ's authority to lead you (Hebrews 13:7) and your response to them must thus be submission in love and obedience as unto God (Hebrews 13:17).

These and more will be explained in subsequent detail in the next chapters to further deepen our understanding of what the church is and the role it plays in the earth today

CHAPTER 2

WHAT THE LOCAL CHURCH IS NOT- (ONLINE CHURCH)

A fruit of Christian maturity or spiritual growth and development is discernment and coming with discernment isn't just the ability to tell apart what is right from what is wrong, it also includes the ability to distil and distinguish between what is nearly right from what is right. This is the case when, as believers or members of a local church, we are presented with a situation wherein we have to ask ourselves sincerely and truthfully if we're not acting like Rehoboam in the scriptures who rather than make the appropriate choices in ministry (that is, in the building of the temple and by extension in the worship/service of God) went on to make convenient ones and ended up substituting "brass for gold". This implies that it is not enough to just want to do the right things (which in this context is to have a proper and biblically defined approach to what the local is or is not), we must also endeavour to do the right things the right way.

> **2 Chronicles 12:1-2** And it came to pass, when Rehoboam had established the kingdom, and had strengthened himself, he forsook the law of the LORD, and all Israel with him. Vs 2 And it came to pass, that in the fifth year of king Rehoboam Shishak king of Egypt came up against Jerusalem, because they had transgressed against the LORD,

> **2 Chronicles 12:9** So Shishak king of Egypt came up against Jerusalem, and took away the treasures of the house of the LORD, and the treasures of the king's house; he took all: he carried away also the shields of gold which Solomon had made.

Observe the story in this text.

Rehoboam became king over God's people, Israel. He left the laws passed to him. In the process, Egypt invaded and took away the valuables in the house of the Lord and in the king's house. Rather than recover them or better still, replace them with exactly what was used in the house handed over to him, he went for expediency

> **2 Chronicles 12:10** Instead of which king Rehoboam made shields of brass, and committed them to the hands of the chief of the guard, that kept the entrance of the king's house.

He used brass.

Brass looks like gold but it is not. We often might fall into the error of doing this with the ministry of our Lord Jesus Christ, that is, we go for what is available, appealing, popular or convenient and not necessarily what is right, scriptural or biblical. This is what has led us to even begin to have a conversation on a non-biblical term such as "the online church", which is being referred to by some as the "new normal" when it comes to the local church and its meetings or gatherings.

Paul warned against this

> **1 Corinthians 3:10-12** According to the grace of God which is given unto me, as a wise masterbuilder, I have laid the foundation, and another buildeth thereon. But let every man take heed how he buildeth thereupon. Vs 11 For other foundation can no man lay than that is laid, which is Jesus Christ. Vs 12 Now if any man build upon this foundation gold, silver, precious stones, wood, hay, stubble;

Instead of precious stones like Paul mentioned, we go for what is available.

Many times, in the name of "meeting needs" or as some might say, "adapting to the times", we side-step scriptures.

This particularly resonates with the advent of the "online church".

Prior to the outbreak of the COVID-19 pandemic across different nations of the world in the year 2020, no one really defined recordings or videos of local church services as them having an online service or church, rather much of these recordings or videos (whether livestreamed or recorded) were simply seen and treated as study tools or opportunities or resources to re-live a meeting that one attended physically or missed out on due to unavoidable circumstances. Infact, many a believer would have counted it as a loss to have been absent at a church meeting of theirs where there was a lot of the teaching of God's word or the "move" of the spirit than to sit back at home to watch or livestream the meetings because deep down within us, we knew that we were better off being physically present at such meetings than being told about what happened there.

Now, coming with the pandemic was the very noble and healthy option to reduce the spread of the virus by reducing the numbers of people congregating in one place at the same time.

This was a scripturally sound option as we see that even in scriptures, isolation or quarantine of people to avoid the spread of diseases was practiced

> **Leviticus 13:1-59** And the LORD spake unto Moses and Aaron, saying, Vs 2 When a man shall have in the skin of his flesh a rising, a scab, or bright spot, and it be in the skin of his flesh like the plague of leprosy; then he

shall be brought unto Aaron the priest, or unto one of his sons the priests: Vs 3 And the priest shall look on the plague in the skin of the flesh: and when the hair in the plague is turned white, and the plague in sight be deeper than the skin of his flesh, it is a plague of leprosy: and the priest shall look on him, and pronounce him unclean. Vs 4 If the bright spot be white in the skin of his flesh, and in sight be not deeper than the skin, and the hair thereof be not turned white; then the priest shall shut up him that hath the plague seven days: Vs 5 And the priest shall look on him the seventh day: and, behold, if the plague in his sight be at a stay, and the plague spread not in the skin; then the priest shall shut him up seven days more: Vs 6 And the priest shall look on him again the seventh day: and, behold, if the plague be somewhat dark, and the plague spread not in the skin, the priest shall pronounce him clean: it is but a scab: and he shall wash his clothes, and be clean. Vs 7 But if the scab spread much abroad in the skin, after that he hath been seen of the priest for his cleansing, he shall be seen of the priest again: Vs 8 And if the priest see that, behold, the scab spreadeth in the skin, then the priest shall pronounce him unclean: it is a leprosy. Vs 9 When the plague of leprosy is in a man, then he shall be brought unto the priest; Vs 10 And the priest shall see him: and, behold, if the rising be white in the skin, and it have turned the hair white, and there be quick raw flesh in the rising; Vs 11 It is an old leprosy in the skin of his flesh, and the priest shall pronounce him unclean, and shall not shut him up: for he is unclean. Vs 12 And if a leprosy break out abroad in the skin, and the leprosy cover all the skin of him that hath the plague from his head even to his foot, wheresoever the priest looketh; Vs 13 Then the priest shall consider: and, behold, if the leprosy have covered all his flesh, he shall pronounce him clean that hath the plague: it is all turned white: he is clean. Vs 14 But when raw flesh appeareth in him, he shall be unclean. Vs 15 And the priest shall see the raw flesh, and pronounce him to be unclean: for the raw flesh is unclean: it is a leprosy. Vs 16 Or if the raw flesh turn again, and be changed unto white, he shall come unto the priest; Vs 17 And the priest shall see him: and, behold, if the plague be turned into white; then the priest shall pronounce him clean that hath the plague: he is clean. Vs 18 The flesh also, in which, even in the skin thereof, was a boil, and is healed, Vs 19 And in the place of the boil there be a white rising, or a bright spot, white, and somewhat reddish, and it be shewed to the priest; Vs 20 And if, when the priest seeth it, behold, it be in sight lower than the skin, and the hair thereof be turned white; the priest shall pronounce him unclean: it is a plague of leprosy broken out of the boil. Vs 21 But if the priest look on it, and, behold, there be no white hairs therein, and if it be not lower than the skin, but be somewhat dark; then the priest shall shut him up seven days: Vs 22 And if it spread much abroad in the skin, then the priest shall pronounce him unclean: it is a plague. Vs 23 But if the bright spot stay in his place, and spread not, it is a burning boil; and the priest shall pronounce him clean.

Vs 24 Or if there be any flesh, in the skin whereof there
is a hot burning, and the quick flesh that burneth have a
white bright spot, somewhat reddish, or white; Vs 25
Then the priest shall look upon it: and, behold, if the
hair in the bright spot be turned white, and it be in sight
deeper than the skin; it is a leprosy broken out of the
burning: wherefore the priest shall pronounce him
unclean: it is the plague of leprosy. Vs 26 But if the
priest look on it, and, behold, there be no white hair in
the bright spot, and it be no lower than the other skin,
but be somewhat dark; then the priest shall shut him up
seven days: Vs 27 And the priest shall look upon him
the seventh day: and if it be spread much abroad in the
skin, then the priest shall pronounce him unclean: it is
the plague of leprosy. Vs 28 And if the bright spot stay
in his place, and spread not in the skin, but it be
somewhat dark; it is a rising of the burning, and the
priest shall pronounce him clean: for it is an
inflammation of the burning. Vs 29 If a man or woman
have a plague upon the head or the beard; Vs 30 Then
the priest shall see the plague: and, behold, if it be in
sight deeper than the skin; and there be in it a yellow
thin hair; then the priest shall pronounce him unclean:
it is a dry scall, even a leprosy upon the head or beard.
Vs 31 And if the priest look on the plague of the scall,
and, behold, it be not in sight deeper than the skin, and
that there is no black hair in it; then the priest shall shut
up him that hath the plague of the scall seven days: Vs
32 And in the seventh day the priest shall look on the
plague: and, behold, if the scall spread not, and there be

in it no yellow hair, and the scall be not in sight deeper than the skin; Vs 33 He shall be shaven, but the scall shall he not shave; and the priest shall shut up him that hath the scall seven days more: Vs 34 And in the seventh day the priest shall look on the scall: and, behold, if the scall be not spread in the skin, nor be in sight deeper than the skin; then the priest shall pronounce him clean: and he shall wash his clothes, and be clean. Vs 35 But if the scall spread much in the skin after his cleansing; Vs 36 Then the priest shall look on him: and, behold, if the scall be spread in the skin, the priest shall not seek for yellow hair; he is unclean. Vs 37 But if the scall be in his sight at a stay, and that there is black hair grown up therein; the scall is healed, he is clean: and the priest shall pronounce him clean. Vs 38 If a man also or a woman have in the skin of their flesh bright spots, even white bright spots; Vs 39 Then the priest shall look: and, behold, if the bright spots in the skin of their flesh be darkish white; it is a freckled spot that groweth in the skin; he is clean. Vs 40 And the man whose hair is fallen off his head, he is bald; yet is he clean. Vs 41 And he that hath his hair fallen off from the part of his head toward his face, he is forehead bald: yet is he clean. Vs 42 And if there be in the bald head, or bald forehead, a white reddish sore; it is a leprosy sprung up in his bald head, or his bald forehead. Vs 43 Then the priest shall look upon it: and, behold, if the rising of the sore be white reddish in his bald head, or in his bald forehead, as the leprosy appeareth in the skin of the flesh; Vs 44 He is a leprous man, he is unclean: the priest shall pronounce him utterly unclean; his plague is in his head. Vs 45 And the leper in whom the plague is, his clothes shall be rent, and his head bare, and he shall put a covering upon his upper lip, and shall cry, Unclean, unclean. Vs 46 All the days wherein the plague shall be in him he shall be defiled; he is unclean: he shall dwell alone; without the camp shall his habitation be. Vs 47 The garment also that the plague of leprosy is in, whether it be a woollen garment, or a linen garment; Vs 48 Whether it be in the warp, or woof; of linen, or of woollen; whether in a skin, or in any thing made of skin; Vs 49 And if the plague be greenish or reddish in the garment, or in the skin, either in the warp, or in the woof, or in any thing of skin; it is a plague of leprosy, and shall be shewed unto the priest: Vs 50 And the priest shall look upon the plague, and shut up it that hath the plague seven days: Vs 51 And he shall look on the plague on the seventh day: if the plague be spread in the garment, either in the warp, or in the woof, or in a skin, or in any work that is made of skin; the plague is a fretting leprosy; it is unclean. Vs 52 He shall therefore burn that garment, whether warp or woof, in woollen or in linen, or any thing of skin, wherein the plague is: for it is a fretting leprosy; it shall be burnt in the fire. Vs 53 And if the priest shall look, and, behold, the plague be not spread in the garment, either in the warp, or in the woof, or in any thing of skin; Vs 54 Then the priest shall command that they wash the thing wherein the plague is, and he shall shut it up seven days more: Vs 55 And the priest shall look on the plague, after that it is washed: and, behold, if the plague have not changed his colour, and the plague be not spread; it is unclean; thou shalt burn it in the fire; it is fret inward, whether it be bare within or without. Vs 56 And if the priest look, and, behold, the plague be somewhat dark after the washing of it; then he shall rend it out of the garment, or out of the skin, or out of the warp, or out of the woof: Vs 57 And if it appear still in the garment, either in the warp, or in the woof, or in any thing of skin; it is a spreading plague: thou shalt burn that wherein the plague is with fire. Vs 58 And the garment, either warp, or woof, or whatsoever thing of skin it be, which thou shalt wash, if the plague be departed from them, then it shall be washed the second time, and shall be clean. Vs 59 This is the law of the plague of leprosy in a garment of woollen or linen, either in the warp, or woof, or any thing of skins, to pronounce it clean, or to pronounce it unclean.

Now, whilst this isolation and quarantine period dragged on and seemed to not want to come to an end, local churches were seemingly put in a dilemma as their members could no longer physically congregate or hold meetings at some point due to governmental laws and restrictions and most resorted to meeting online to pray, to study or simply just fellowship with one another.

No doubt that most clergy and laity or local churches that did this were genuine and of noble intent, particularly as many wanted to just "keep the fire burning" in their members one way or another.

However, what was not clearly said or explained to many was that this was an expediency of that time, one which naturally should have expired with the expiration of the pandemic and its restrictions.

Thus, what should have ideally led to a situation where believers who had been unable to meet physically for a while and as such should troop into their local church in large numbers after the ban on physical gatherings were lifted, now led to many believers beginning to redefine church and think that God was actually teaching the body of Christ a new or more effective way to have church meetings

To make matters worse, some clergy bought into this (especially as some thought it was an opportunity to grow their following) and many members began to side-step the very clear instructions of scriptures for us not to forsake the assembling of one another.

Now, to be clear, the scriptures' instructions for us to gather or assemble were emphatic about physical gatherings not online gatherings or meetings in any format or platform we can invent

By the etymology and history of the word church or local church, we have no evidence to sustain the practice of the concept of an online church

Etymologically, recall that the word 'church' was translated from the Greek word "ekklesia." We had also established in previous studies that the word "ekklesia' wasn't a word that was created by the Lord Jesus. Rather, he employed the use of that word which was in regular everyday use to describe his church. Ekklesia was the lawful assembly of Greek citizens who met to transact public affairs. Ekklesia is a compound word that was developed from:

- Ek, which means out of
- Kaleo, which means to call or to summon

The word "ekklesia" has its historic origins from the Hebrew word 'synagoge.' The latter (to its Greek audience) meant any gathering or bringing together of persons or things. The word 'synagogue' was also used to describe set apart places of worship where the Hebrew scriptures were read and expounded to the audience. The multiplied places of worship that the synagogue represented were seen in their existence to be complementary to the Jewish temple.

From the foregoing, it is clear that the word 'ekklesia' had its origins in the secular world. It bears mentioning that the Septuagint translated 'edah[4]' as 'synagoge.' The word qahal[5] on the other hand was a bit more fluid in its

---

[4] In the Authorized Version was translated as congregation (Leviticus 10:17, Numbers 1:16, Joshua 9:27) and also as assembly (Leviticus 4:13)

translation to the Greek language. In some instances, it was translated as 'ekklesia,' and in some others as 'synagoge.'

Vitringa gives us something to think about as he makes a distinction between these two Hebrew synonyms.

> "Qahal, strictly speaking, denotes an entire multitude of some people united by the bonds of society and making up a republic or a certain state, while the word edah, from the nature and force of its emphasis, speaks of only any assembly and gathering of people, whether small or large[6]."

In the same material, he says:

Synagoge, as also edah, always signifies an assembly joined and gathered together, although bound by no strong bond; but the ekklesia [= qahal] designates some multitude which makes up a people joined together by laws and bonds, although frequently they may happen not to be assembled or are not able to be assembled[7].

This distinction may have resulted in why the translators opted for ekklesia over edah.

---

[5] Sometimes translated as assembly (Judges 21:8, 2 Chronicles 30:23)
[6] De synagoga vetere, p.80
[7] De synagoga vetere, p.88

Matthew 16:18 And I say also unto thee, That thou art Peter, and upon this rock I will build my **church**; and the gates of hell shall not prevail against it.

His personalization of the word 'ekklesia' would be a pointer to Jesus being the founder of this family bound by the spirit and whose reach would be in every inhabited space on earth.

The Great Commission in Mark 16 comes to mind, and rightly so.

Mark 16:15 And he said unto them, Go ye into all the world, and preach the gospel to every creature.

Considering that culture informs language and its use of words, it bears with reason that since the word 'ekklesia' had a more honourable meaning than edah, it would as a result clearly take precedence in their writings.

It bears mentioning however that the word 'synagogue' was translated as **assembly** by the apostle James in his epistle[8]. His reference was to a physical gathering.

---

[8] The only other writer in the epistles who applied the word synagogue was John in the book of Revelation. It was applied in reference to the gathering of Jews who opposed the truth - Revelation 2:9, Revelation 3:9. It seemingly thus appears that the use of the word 'synagoge' for the assembling of believers petered out over time.

James 2:2 For if there come unto your **assembly** a man with a gold ring, in goodly apparel, and there come in also a poor man in vile raiment;

That word forms a part of the compound word 'episunagoge' which was applied twice in New Testament writings.

2 Thessalonians 2:1 Now we beseech you, brethren, by the **coming** of our Lord Jesus Christ, and by our **gathering together** unto him,

Observe that it was applied in close relation to the word 'parousia.'

Hebrews 10:25 Not forsaking **the assembling** of ourselves **together**, as the manner of some is; but exhorting one another: and so much the more, as ye see the day approaching.

Such is the force of the word 'episunagoge' that the writer of the book of Hebrews applied it twice in the same sentence. Might we say, not forsaking the assembling of ourselves assembling, or the together of ourselves together.

One thing is very clear, he promotes that gathering of believers and instructs a regularity to it.

1 Timothy 3:15 But if I tarry long, that thou mayest know how thou oughtest to behave thyself in the **house**

of God, which is the church of the living God, the pillar and ground of the truth.

The word 'house' was translated from a word that means family; a household. Hence, the family of God is the church of the living God. It is God's family. It is a supernatural assembly. In Luke's account in the book of Acts, he makes an allusion to that gathering.

Furthermore, the word 'congregation' is used 14 times in the book of Exodus, 12 times in Leviticus, 83 times in the book of Numbers, 15 times in Joshua, 5 times in Judges, 2 times in 1 Kings, once in 2 Chronicles, twice in Job, 10 times in the Psalms, once in the book of Proverbs, twice in Jeremiah and once in Hosea. That congregation is effective in the assembly; in the gatherings.

ITS USAGE IN THE BOOK OF EXODUS

Exodus 12:6 And ye shall keep it up until the fourteenth day of the same month: and the **whole assembly** of the **congregation** of Israel shall kill it in the evening… Vs 19 Seven days shall there be no leaven found in your houses: for whosoever eateth that which is leavened, even that soul shall be cut off from the **congregation** of Israel, whether he be a stranger, or born in the land… Vs 47 **All** the **congregation** of Israel shall keep it.

Exodus 16:1 And they took their journey from Elim, and **all** the **congregation** of the children of Israel came unto the wilderness of Sin, which is between Elim and Sinai, on the fifteenth day of the second month after their departing out of the land of Egypt. **Vs 2** And the **whole congregation** of the children of Israel murmured against Moses and Aaron in the wilderness… **Vs 9** And Moses spake unto Aaron, Say unto **all the congregation** of the children of Israel, Come near before the Lord: for he hath heard your murmurings. **Vs 10** And it came to pass, as Aaron spake unto **the whole congregation** of the children of Israel, that they looked toward the wilderness, and, behold, the glory of the Lord appeared in the cloud… **Vs 22** And it came to pass, that on the sixth day they gathered twice as much bread, two omers for one man: and all the rulers of **the congregation** came and told Moses.

Exodus 17:1 And **all the congregation** of the children of Israel journeyed from the wilderness of Sin, after their journeys, according to the commandment of the Lord, and pitched in Rephidim: and there was no water for the people to drink.

Observe words used with the congregation: whole assembly, the, all. Observe it refers to everyone in the assembly of the children of Israel and is functional in the gatherings as a singular, indivisible unit.

Its shades of meaning include an assembly, a family, a multitude, a crowd, a company, a swarm.

Observe that in the worship of God, the primary activity that was obtainable in the congregation was the teaching of the laws and statutes of God.

> **Exodus 18:12** And Jethro, Moses' father in law, took a burnt offering and sacrifices for God: and Aaron came, and all the elders of Israel, to eat bread with Moses' father in law before God. **Vs 13** And it came to pass on the morrow, that **Moses sat to judge the people: and the people stood by Moses from the morning unto the evening**. **Vs 14** And when Moses' father in law saw all that he did to the people, he said, What is this thing that thou doest to the people? why sittest thou thyself alone, and all the people stand by thee from morning unto even? **Vs 15** And Moses said unto his father in law, Because **the people come unto me to enquire of God**: **Vs 16** When they have a matter, they come unto me; and **I judge between one and another, and I do make them know the statutes of God, and his laws**.

Observe also another fact that emerged from the assembly. Jethro, Moses' father-in-law counselled him to raise leaders from among the people.

> **Exodus 18:17** And Moses' father in law said unto him, The thing that thou doest is not good. Vs 18 Thou wilt surely wear away, both thou, and this people that is with thee: for this thing is too heavy for thee; thou art not able to perform it thyself alone. Vs 19 Hearken now unto my voice, I will give thee counsel, and God shall

be with thee: Be thou for the people to God-ward, that thou mayest bring the causes unto God: Vs 20 And thou shalt teach them ordinances and laws, and shalt shew them the way wherein they must walk, and the work that they must do. **Vs 21** Moreover **thou shalt provide out of all the people able men, such as fear God, men of truth, hating covetousness;** and place such over them, to be rulers of thousands, and rulers of hundreds, rulers of fifties, and rulers of tens: Vs 22 And let them judge the people at all seasons: and it shall be, that every great matter they shall bring unto thee, but every small matter they shall judge: so shall it be easier for thyself, and they shall bear the burden with thee. Vs 23 If thou shalt do this thing, and God command thee so, then thou shalt be able to endure, and all this people shall also go to their place in peace. Vs 24 So Moses hearkened to the voice of his father in law, and did all that he had said.

Consider Exodus 18:21 from other translations

Exodus 18:21 Moreover thou shalt provide out of all the people able men, **such as fear God, men of truth, hating covetousness**; and place such over them, to be rulers of thousands, and rulers of hundreds, rulers of fifties, and rulers of tens: (ESV)

Exodus 18:21 Moreover, look for able men from all the people, **men who fear God, who are trustworthy and hate a bribe**, and place such men over the people as chiefs of thousands, of hundreds, of fifties, and of tens. (ESV)

Exodus 18:21 But select from all the people some capable, honest men who fear God and hate bribes. Appoint them as leaders over groups of one thousand, one hundred, fifty, and ten. (NLT)

Exodus 18:21 And then you need to keep a sharp eye out for **competent men - men who fear God, men of integrity, men who are incorruptible** - and appoint them as leaders over groups organized by the thousand, by the hundred, by fifty, and by ten. (MSG)

Exodus 18:21 But you should select from all the people **able men, God-fearing, trustworthy, and hating bribes.** Place [them] over the people as officials of thousands, hundreds, fifties, and tens. (CSB)

In response to Jethro's counsel, Moses chose able men out of all Israel. These were men that he could train and who could share the burden of leadership with him.

Exodus 18:25 And Moses chose able men out of all Israel, and made them heads over the people, rulers of thousands, rulers of hundreds, rulers of fifties, and rulers of tens. **Vs 26** And **they judged the people at all seasons**: the hard causes they brought unto Moses, but every small matter they judged themselves.

There was thus a multiplicity of leadership among the people.

The account in Numbers 11 provides a further glimpse into the development of leadership among the congregation.

> **Numbers 11:10** Then Moses heard the people weep throughout their families, every man in the door of his tent: and the anger of the Lord was kindled greatly; Moses also was displeased. Vs 11 And Moses said unto the Lord, Wherefore hast thou afflicted thy servant? and wherefore have I not found favour in thy sight, that thou layest the burden of all this people upon me? Vs 12 Have I conceived all this people? have I begotten them, that thou shouldest say unto me, Carry them in thy bosom, as a nursing father beareth the sucking child, unto the land which thou swarest unto their fathers? Vs 13 Whence should I have flesh to give unto all this people? for they weep unto me, saying, Give us flesh, that we may eat. Vs 14 **I am not able to bear all this people alone**, because it is too heavy for me. Vs 15 And if thou deal thus with me, kill me, I pray thee, out of hand, if I have found favour in thy sight; and let me not see my wretchedness. Vs 16 And the Lord said unto Moses, **Gather unto me seventy men of the elders of Israel, whom thou knowest to be the elders of the people, and officers over them**; and bring them unto the tabernacle of **the congregation**, that they may stand there with thee.

Observe that the choosing of the elders was not some random exercise. Their being put in office happened in the congregation of the people in the tabernacle, in what you might describe as the church gatherings or meetings.

That said, let's consider the use of the word church or local church from the historical perspective of the emergence of the local church in the book of Acts. Historically, a closer look into the book of Acts (the emergence of the church) and the epistles should further show us with clarity what the local church is and what it is not

> **Acts 1:4-8** And, being assembled together with them, commanded them that they should not depart from Jerusalem, but wait for the promise of the Father, which, saith he, ye have heard of me. Vs 5 For John truly baptized with water; but ye shall be baptized with the Holy Ghost not many days hence. Vs 6 When they therefore were come together, they asked of him, saying, Lord, wilt thou at this time restore again the kingdom to Israel? Vs 7 And he said unto them, It is not for you to know the times or the seasons, which the Father hath put in his own power. Vs 8 But ye shall receive power, after that the Holy Ghost is come upon you: and ye shall be witnesses unto me both in Jerusalem, and in all Judaea, and in Samaria, and unto the uttermost part of the earth.

Notice that in verse 4, Jesus "assembled" with them and then gave them clear instructions not to depart from Jerusalem (a definite place and physical gathering). They were to be endued with power from on high and this did not happen to them online or individually but in a collective and physical gathering. Infact, the disciples were recorded to have stayed together in one accord in prayer and supplication until this happened which implies that they were literal and big on physical gatherings

> **Acts 1:14** These all continued with one accord in prayer and supplication, with the women, and Mary the mother of Jesus, and with his brethren.

Again, it is quite instructive to note that Luke records in this same chapter that a major criteria for which Matthias was chosen as a replacement apostle in the stead of Judas was that he was with them (an obvious reference to being physically present and not by proxy) at all times from the very beginning, that is, just like the other 11 apostles that Jesus chose to "be with him", Matthias was in every meeting that Jesus had

> **Acts 1:21-22** Wherefore of these men which have companied with us all the time that the Lord Jesus went in and out among us, Vs 22 Beginning from the baptism of John, unto that same day that he was taken up from us, must one be ordained to be a witness with us of his resurrection.

Furthermore, when Peter and the 11 apostles preached on the day of Pentecost in Acts 2, we notice that about three thousand souls were added unto them but what was even more instructive about this was that despite the fact that this men came from different places to Jerusalem to celebrate Pentecost, they understood that there was "no church" without them staying back to gather with the apostles and disciples to continue in the apostles' doctrine and fellowship

> **Acts 2:40-42** And with many other words did he testify and exhort, saying, Save yourselves from this untoward generation. Vs 41 Then they that gladly received his word were baptized: and the same day there were added unto them about three thousand souls. Vs 42 And they continued stedfastly in the apostles' doctrine and fellowship, and in breaking of bread, and in prayers.

> **Acts 2:46-47** And they, continuing daily with one accord in the temple, and breaking bread from house to house, did eat their meat with gladness and singleness of heart, Vs 47 Praising God, and having favour with all the people. And the Lord added to the church daily such as should be saved.

They continued daily in one accord and met in the temple (literally or physically) and the Lord kept adding to them

For the avoidance of doubt, a viable option and technology of their day was to ask them all to go back home and "do church' via hand-written letters or epistles from the apostles on a daily or weekly basis

Let's proceed to the next chapter and see if they continued or sustained this practice of physical church meetings or gatherings

In Acts 3, we see that the church not only continued to meet, they also had clearly defined meetings such that we see Peter and John go up together into the temple at the hour of prayer

Acts 3 verse 1

That means they had what we can call prayer meetings. This prayer meeting led to another outreach or evangelistic meeting (the first being that of Acts 2) where a man who was crippled from birth received healing and many others were taught and had Jesus' resurrection preached to them such that another five thousand souls were added to them

> **Acts 4:1-4** And as they spake unto the people, the priests, and the captain of the temple, and the Sadducees, came upon them, Vs 2 Being grieved that they taught the people, and preached through Jesus the resurrection from the dead. Vs 3 And they laid hands on them, and put them in hold unto the next day: for it was now eventide. Vs 4 Howbeit many of them which heard the word believed; and the number of the men was about five thousand.

Observe as well that when the apostles here were threatened, they returned to their own company (their local church) which mathematically speaking was now a local church of no less than about eight thousand people and they gathered together (physically) to pray for boldness, signs and wonders to be done as they preached the gospel

Again, a convenient option here would have been to try to reach Jerusalem with the gospel "online" or anonymously or subtly via letters but they kept gathering together and even became bolder about this

> **Acts 4:24-33** And when they heard that, they lifted up their voice to God with one accord, and said, Lord, thou art God, which hast made heaven, and earth, and the sea, and all that in them is: Vs 25 Who by the mouth of thy servant David hast said, Why did the heathen rage, and the people imagine vain things? Vs 26 The kings of the earth stood up, and the rulers were gathered together against the Lord, and against his Christ. Vs 27 For of a truth against thy holy child Jesus, whom thou hast anointed, both Herod, and Pontius Pilate, with the Gentiles, and the people of Israel, were gathered together, Vs 28 For to do whatsoever thy hand and thy counsel determined before to be done. Vs 29 And now, Lord, behold their threatenings: and grant unto thy servants, that with all boldness they may speak thy word, Vs 30 By stretching forth thine hand to heal; and that signs and wonders may be done by the name of thy

holy child Jesus. Vs 31 And when they had prayed, the place was shaken where they were assembled together; and they were all filled with the Holy Ghost, and they spake the word of God with boldness. Vs 32 And the multitude of them that believed were of one heart and of one soul: neither said any of them that ought of the things which he possessed was his own; but they had all things common. Vs 33 And with great power gave the apostles witness of the resurrection of the Lord Jesus: and great grace was upon them all.

In Acts 5, Luke records the Ananias and Sapphira incidence which strongly indicates that this local church had definite leadership and a structure for accountability even with respect to giving. He goes further to show that the believers were all with one accord in Solomon's porch, that is, this was definitely no online service or church meeting but a very physical and relational one

Acts 5:12 And by the hands of the apostles were many signs and wonders wrought among the people; (and they were all with one accord in Solomon's porch.

In verse 14, observe again the emphasis on believers being added to them, multitudes both of men and women in an obviously physical gathering or assembly. In verse 42, Luke lets us see that this local church met in large numbers (in the temple) and as well in lesser numbers (from house to house) but they definitely were meeting physically to teach and preach Jesus Christ

In Acts 6, we see again a clear reminder about what the local church is and what it should never be, that is, the apostles stuck to the primary purpose of the ministry of the word and prayer and refused to be distracted or side-stepped into just focusing on welfarism or just "meeting people's need". Also, notice that the multitudes were referred to as disciples which means that there was massive discipleship going on such that it was possible to pick out seven men who had these sterling qualities and were made deacons. These men were initially chosen to serve tables but it was obvious that they were good disciples of the apostles who were full of the Holy ghost and could handle God's word intelligently as was seen in Stephen all through chapter 7

> **Acts 6:1-8** And in those days, when the number of the disciples was multiplied, there arose a murmuring of the Grecians against the Hebrews, because their widows were neglected in the daily ministration. Vs 2 Then the twelve called the multitude of the disciples unto them, and said, It is not reason that we should leave the word of God, and serve tables. Vs 3 Wherefore, brethren, look ye out among you seven men of honest report, full of the Holy Ghost and wisdom, whom we may appoint over this business. Vs 4 But we will give ourselves continually to prayer, and to the ministry of the word. Vs 5 And the saying pleased the whole multitude: and they chose Stephen, a man full of faith and of the Holy Ghost, and Philip, and Prochorus, and Nicanor, and Timon, and Parmenas, and Nicolas a

> proselyte of Antioch: Vs 6 Whom they set before the apostles: and when they had prayed, they laid their hands on them. Vs 7 And the word of God increased; and the number of the disciples multiplied in Jerusalem greatly; and a great company of the priests were obedient to the faith. Vs 8 And Stephen, full of faith and power, did great wonders and miracles among the people.

By Acts 8, upon Stephen's death, there was a great persecution in Jerusalem that eventually scattered the disciples abroad (except the apostles) yet they went everywhere preaching the word and ultimately, this was how other local churches (gatherings of believers) emerged or developed in the places they went to. For instance, we see Philip in Samaria, he preached the gospel to the whole city and called on the apostles in Jerusalem to come over to get them filled and consequently endorse what he was doing there.

In Acts 9, Luke again shows us that the church had local church meetings or gatherings such that Saul (Paul) could say he was going to the synagogues in Damascus to bind anyone he found as disciples of the Lord Jesus

> **Acts 9:1-2** And Saul, yet breathing out threatenings and slaughter against the disciples of the Lord, went unto the high priest, Vs 2 And desired of him letters to Damascus to the synagogues, that if he found any of

> this way, whether they were men or women, he might bring them bound unto Jerusalem.

In verse 10, we read of Ananias, a certain disciple at Damascus who must have been well taught and also well known by his local church such that he not only related well with the Lord Jesus in a vision but went on to carry out Jesus' instructions and laid hands on Saul to get him filled with the Spirit and for him to recover his sight. In this same account is shown to us a very outstanding truth about the church and the local church in that upon Saul's conversion (faith in Christ), he was immediately referred to as "Brother Saul" and subsequently introduced into the assembly of believers. He spent certain days with the disciples at Damascus and straightway began to preach Christ in the synagogues. Notice as well that the local church there protected him and kept him away from harm and eventually sent him to Jerusalem. On getting to Jerusalem, Barnabas took him, endorsed and vouched for him and helped him to be received into the local church there before he was again sent forth to Tarsus for his safety

> **Acts 9:17-30** And Ananias went his way, and entered into the house; and putting his hands on him said, Brother Saul, the Lord, even Jesus, that appeared unto thee in the way as thou camest, hath sent me, that thou mightest receive thy sight, and be filled with the Holy Ghost. Vs 18 And immediately there fell from his eyes as it had been scales: and he received sight forthwith, and arose, and was baptized. Vs 19 And when he had

received meat, he was strengthened. Then was Saul certain days with the disciples which were at Damascus. Vs 20 And straightway he preached Christ in the synagogues, that he is the Son of God. Vs 21 But all that heard him were amazed, and said; Is not this he that destroyed them which called on this name in Jerusalem, and came hither for that intent, that he might bring them bound unto the chief priests? Vs 22 But Saul increased the more in strength, and confounded the Jews which dwelt at Damascus, proving that this is very Christ. Vs 23 And after that many days were fulfilled, the Jews took counsel to kill him: Vs 24 But their laying await was known of Saul. And they watched the gates day and night to kill him. Vs 25 Then the disciples took him by night, and let him down by the wall in a basket. Vs 26 And when Saul was come to Jerusalem, he assayed to join himself to the disciples: but they were all afraid of him, and believed not that he was a disciple. Vs 27 But Barnabas took him, and brought him to the apostles, and declared unto them how he had seen the Lord in the way, and that he had spoken to him, and how he had preached boldly at Damascus in the name of Jesus. Vs 28 And he was with them coming in and going out at Jerusalem. Vs 29 And he spake boldly in the name of the Lord Jesus, and disputed against the Grecians: but they went about to slay him. Vs 30 Which when the brethren knew, they brought him down to Caesarea, and sent him forth to Tarsus.

The emphasis on the local church(es) and physical gatherings or meetings continued to replay itself all through the chapters of the book of Acts

In chapter 12, we see believers gather together in one place for prayer meetings dedicated for the deliverance of Peter

In Acts 13, we see a ministers' meeting and subsequently Paul and Barnabas were sent forth on a missionary journey and everywhere they went they kept raising disciples and birthing or pioneering local assemblies with the gospel of Christ

Acts 14 verse 21 - 23 is also quite instructive:

> **Acts 14:21-23** And when they had preached the gospel to that city, and had taught many, they returned again to Lystra, and to Iconium, and Antioch, Vs 22 Confirming the souls of the disciples, and exhorting them to continue in the faith, and that we must through much tribulation enter into the kingdom of God. Vs 23 And when they had ordained them elders in every church, and had prayed with fasting, they commended them to the Lord, on whom they believed.

Here we see that they spent time to strengthen disciples via exhortations and actually ordained elders (spiritually matured believers) in every church (local assemblies) that they planted or pioneered which shows that people were not just being saved and left "to know Jesus on their own" rather they were being discipled and handed over to proper church leadership for spiritual growth and nurturing.

Acts 15 shows us that there was the viable science and technology option of their day in writing of letters and this was deployed when necessary to settle a major doctrinal dispute or debate amongst the local churches then. However, notice that those letters were delivered personally by Paul, Barnabas and some others as recommended by the apostles and elders in the church in Jerusalem. This means that the letters still did not replace physical teaching meetings wherein the brethren were exhorted by Judas and Silas who were prophets

Much can still be said of all of Paul's missionary journeys and how in pioneering local churches in different places, he would spend time to teach, nurture and raise disciples, sometimes doing this daily for the space of two years (as was recorded in Acts 19 verse 10) and sometimes doing this all day and all night, labouring in teaching meetings to declare unto them the whole counsel of God, publicly and from house to house.

> **Acts 20:20** And how I kept back nothing that was profitable unto you, but have shewed you, and have taught you publickly, and from house to house,

> **Acts 20:27** For I have not shunned to declare unto you all the counsel of God.

Even in incarceration and eventually till his death, Luke records that Paul kept on holding teaching meetings (despite writing letters to remind and strengthen them on the things he had taught them whilst he was physically present with them)

> **Acts 28:30-31** And Paul dwelt two whole years in his own hired house, and received all that came in unto him, Vs 31 Preaching the kingdom of God, and teaching those things which concern the Lord Jesus Christ, with all confidence, no man forbidding him.

Christianity is apostolic and historical, which means that what we believe and practice today as the Christian faith can actually be traced to certain men in history. Hence, what we have done so far in this chapter, in defining what the local church is and what it is not, is to look at the etymology of the word church and/or the local church and also to retrace our steps back to the birth of the church in the book of acts and juxtapose their practices with our time and see if we can find any synonym or background for what is today referred to as online church or services. This study has so far presented to us no evidence of such, whether literally or impliedly, rather what we see is unassailable evidence and strong emphasis on the local church carrying out its tasks of discipleship and training of believers via physical gatherings.

However, some may argue that what we have after the book of Acts are called epistles, which means that the apostles made use of the technology of their day to reach or teach believers. For instance, Paul wrote about 13 of these, followed by the writer of the book of Hebrews, then James' letter to the twelve tribes scattered abroad, then Peter wrote 2 letters, John wrote 3, Jude wrote 1 and then the book of the revelation of Jesus as received and recorded by John.

Does this suffice as background or a defence for an online church?

Let's find out by thorough examination: Firstly, Luke shows us in the book of Acts as we have seen earlier that the pattern of the apostles in writing letters was to use those letters as "follow-up" materials on what they had earlier taught in physical gatherings either in large meetings in their synagogues or in "house fellowship" meetings. This means, those letters were not their first contact with those believers (except in the case of the church in Colosse that Paul was said to have pioneered through Epaphras his disciple) and as such those letters were never designed to replace physical gatherings and were in fact designed to strengthen physical gatherings as many times the letters were written to congregations not individuals, that is, they were written to be read in the local churches in those places which meant that you had to be in church when those letters were read and often re-explained by the leaders of those local churches

Colossians 4:16 And when this epistle is read among you, cause that it be read also in the church of the Laodiceans; and that ye likewise read the epistle from Laodicea.

Notice that this epistle was read in or to a physical gathering and they were doing the same thing in the local church(es) in Laodicea.

Furthermore, we have evidence in those letter or epistles that the writers, despite having the opportunity to write to people in their absence, longed for and looked forward more to physical meetings or interactions with fellow believers for impartations, stirrings or refreshings

Romans 1:9-12 For God is my witness, whom I serve with my spirit in the gospel of his Son, that without ceasing I make mention of you always in my prayers; Vs 10 Making request, if by any means now at length I might have a prosperous journey by the will of God to come unto you. Vs 11 For I long to see you, that I may impart unto you some spiritual gift, to the end ye may be established; Vs 12 That is, that I may be comforted together with you by the mutual faith both of you and me.

2 Corinthians 2:1-4 But I determined this with myself, that I would not come again to you in heaviness. Vs 2 For if I make you sorry, who is he then that maketh me glad, but the same which is made sorry by me? Vs 3 And I wrote this same unto you, lest, when I came, I should have sorrow from them of whom I ought to rejoice; having confidence in you all, that my joy is the joy of you all. Vs 4 For out of much affliction and anguish of heart I wrote unto you with many tears; not that ye should be grieved, but that ye might know the love which I have more abundantly unto you.

2 Corinthians 13:1 This is the third time I am coming to you. In the mouth of two or three witnesses shall every word be established.

In some cases, despite having written letters, Paul would send trusted and capable hands to teach, correct and instruct believers in those local churches, again placing emphasis on physical gathering as an important aspect of discipleship, training and nurturing. This isn't far-fetched when juxtaposed with today's world or realities such that despite the luxury of technology and advancements, no one trains soldiers online. No one gets married and live as couples or make babies online. All of these still place an undying emphasis on physical meetings or interactions and show that online meetings are secondary tools to be used when necessary but never to replace or substitute physical meetings or relations.

Recall, an unchanging, evergreen truth that is fundamental to this study is this: God's method is man. This means that in the workings of God among men, he will use man to reach man. It is the template that he has always worked with.

> **Numbers 11:17** And I will come down and talk with thee there: and I will take of the spirit which is upon thee, and will put it upon them; and they shall bear the burden of the people with thee, that thou bear it not thyself alone.

I will take of the spirit which is upon thee, and will put it upon them.

Observe from the text above that God was going to "multiply" Moses in the lives of the men he was going to choose from among the people.

A key fact to reiterate is the fact that God's method is Man. That is God's way of doing things in the earth. It should provide the believer with much to think about in how we appreciate God's gift that he has put and continues to put in Believers all around us.

There is much to learn in the workings of supernatural relationships developed between certain key personalities in the scriptures. We will consider a number of them in this study:

- Moses and Joshua
- Eli and Samuel
- Paul and Timothy
- The Lord Jesus and the apostles

MOSES AND JOSHUA

Numbers 13:3 And Moses by the commandment of the Lord sent them from the wilderness of Paran: all those men were heads of the children of Israel. Vs 4 And these were their names: of the tribe of Reuben, Shammua the son of Zaccur. Vs 5 Of the tribe of Simeon, Shaphat the son of Hori. Vs 6 Of the tribe of Judah, Caleb the son of Jephunneh. Vs 7 Of the tribe of Issachar, Igal the son of Joseph. Vs 8 **Of the tribe of Ephraim, Oshea the son of Nun.** Vs 9 Of the tribe of Benjamin, Palti the son of Raphu. Vs 10 Of the tribe of Zebulun, Gaddiel the son of Sodi. Vs 11 Of the tribe of Joseph, namely, of the tribe of Manasseh, Gaddi the son of Susi. Vs 12 Of the tribe of Dan, Ammiel the son of Gemalli. Vs 13 Of the tribe of Asher, Sethur the son of Michael. Vs 14 Of the tribe of Naphtali, Nahbi the son of Vophsi. Vs 15 Of the tribe of Gad, Geuel the son of Machi. Vs 16 These are the names of the men which Moses sent to spy out the land. **And Moses called Oshea the son of Nun Jehoshua.**

Joshua was from the tribe of Ephraim. He was one of the spies chosen by Moses to spy out the land that they were going to.

Exodus 17:8 Then came Amalek, and fought with Israel in Rephidim. Vs 9 **And Moses said unto Joshua, Choose us out men, and go out, fight with Amalek**: to morrow I will stand on the top of the hill with the rod of God in mine hand. Vs 10 So **Joshua did as Moses had said to him**, and fought with Amalek: and Moses, Aaron, and Hur went up to the top of the hill. Vs 11 And it came to pass, when Moses held up his hand, that Israel prevailed: and when he let down his hand, Amalek prevailed. Vs 12 But Moses hands were heavy; and they took a stone, and put it under him, and he sat thereon; and Aaron and Hur stayed up his hands, the one on the one side, and the other on the other side; and his hands were steady until the going down of the sun. Vs 13 **And Joshua discomfited Amalek and his people with the edge of the sword.**

The above account also shows a few things that we can learn from in their relationship. He obeyed instructions. He was one who was used to being told what to do by his leader; Moses. He got the job done, just as he was told to. We see echoes of a student; a learner; a disciple.

He served Moses. There are various accounts of his service to Moses.

Numbers 11:27 And there ran a young man, and told Moses, and said, Eldad and Medad do prophesy in the camp. Vs 28 And Joshua the son of Nun, **the servant of Moses, one of his young men**, answered and said, **My lord Moses,** forbid them. Vs 29 And Moses said unto him, Enviest thou for my sake? would God that all the Lord's people were prophets, and that the Lord would put his spirit upon them!

He was described as one of Moses' young men. There was clearly a mentor-mentee relationship at play here. And it was one that functioned with both men relating with each other at close quarters. See how he describes Moses. He uses words that are weighty- My lord Moses.

> **Exodus 24:12** And the Lord said unto Moses, Come up to me into the mount, and be there: and I will give thee tables of stone, and a law, and commandments which I have written; that thou mayest teach them. **Vs 13 And Moses rose up, and his minister Joshua:** and Moses went up into the mount of God. Vs 14 And he said unto the elders, Tarry ye here for us, until we come again unto you: and, behold, Aaron and Hur are with you: if any man have any matters to do, let him come unto them. Vs 15 And Moses went up into the mount, and a cloud covered the mount. Vs 16 **And the glory of the Lord abode upon mount Sinai, and the cloud covered it six days: and the seventh day he called unto Moses out of the midst of the cloud.** Vs 17 And the sight of the glory of the Lord was like devouring fire on the top of the mount in the eyes of the children of Israel. Vs 18 And Moses went into the midst of the cloud, and gat him up into the mount: and Moses was in the mount **forty days and forty nights.**

See how he was described in verse 13- Moses' minister. He took on the identity of the one that he served. He observed him closely.

Exodus 32:17 And when Joshua heard the noise of the people as they shouted, **he said unto Moses, There is a noise of war in the camp.** Vs 18 And he said, It is not the voice of them that shout for mastery, neither is it the voice of them that cry for being overcome: but the noise of them that sing do I hear.

He was one who was given to bringing reports to Moses.

Exodus 33:7 And Moses took the tabernacle, and pitched it without the camp, afar off from the camp, and called it the Tabernacle of the congregation. And it came to pass, that every one which sought the Lord went out unto the tabernacle of the congregation, which was without the camp. Vs 8 And it came to pass, when Moses went out unto the tabernacle, that all the people rose up, and stood every man at his tent door, and looked after Moses, until he was gone into the tabernacle. Vs 9 And it came to pass, as Moses entered into the tabernacle, the cloudy pillar descended, and stood at the door of the tabernacle, and the Lord talked with Moses. Vs 10 And all the people saw the cloudy pillar stand at the tabernacle door: and all the people rose up and worshipped, every man in his tent door. **Vs 11 And the Lord spake unto Moses face to face, as a man speaketh unto his friend. And he turned again into the camp: but his servant Joshua, the son of Nun, a young man, departed not out of the tabernacle.**

In the above account, it appears that Joshua is understudying Moses as he is with him all the time. This has echoes of Mark 3:14.

Observe the words that are used to describe him- his servant Joshua, the son of Nun. In the hierarchy of how he was described, his service to Moses took precedence over his tribal allegiances as the son of Nun. He was also described as a young man. Little wonder, he was chosen by Moses to fill his really big shoes. He succeeded Moses.

> **Numbers 27:15** And Moses spake unto the Lord, saying, Vs 16 Let the Lord, the God of the spirits of all flesh, **set a man over the congregation, Vs** 17 Which may go out before them, and which may go in before them, and which may lead them out, and which may bring them in; **that the congregation of the Lord be not as sheep which have no shepherd**. Vs 18 And the Lord said unto Moses, Take thee Joshua the son of Nun, a man in whom is the spirit, and **lay thine hand upon him**... Vs 23 And **he laid his hands upon him,** and gave him a charge, as the Lord commanded by the hand of Moses.

He is described as a man in whom is the spirit. He is to be Israel's shepherd, servant-leader after Moses. Hands were laid on him to commission him to oversee the lives of the people, just like Moses before him.

> **Deuteronomy 34:9** And Joshua the son of Nun was full of the spirit of wisdom; for Moses had laid his hands

upon him: and the children of Israel hearkened unto him, and did as the Lord commanded Moses.

He was full of the spirit of wisdom because Moses had laid hands on him. This was a result of a close, personal, onsite relationship. Observe that hands were laid on him. In other words, that relationship also provided avenues for impartation of what was upon Moses' life into his. He clearly learnt from what Moses did. He learnt from Moses' experience and he used them. A case in point was when Moses sent out spies to check out the land of Canaan in Numbers 13. Observe that the spies spoke directly to everyone when they arrived.

Numbers 13:25 And they returned from searching of the land after forty days. Vs 26 And they went and came to Moses, and to Aaron, and to all the congregation of the children of Israel, unto the wilderness of Paran, to Kadesh; and brought back word unto them, and unto all the congregation, and shewed them the fruit of the land. Vs 27 And they told him, and said, We came unto the land whither thou sentest us, and surely it floweth with milk and honey; and this is the fruit of it. Vs 28 Nevertheless the people be strong that dwell in the land, and the cities are walled, and very great: and moreover we saw the children of Anak there. Vs 29 The Amalekites dwell in the land of the south: and the Hittites, and the Jebusites, and the Amorites, dwell in the mountains: and the Canaanites dwell by the sea, and by the coast of Jordan. Vs 30 And

Caleb stilled the people before Moses, and said, Let us go up at once, and possess it; for we are well able to overcome it. Vs 31 But the men that went up with him said, We be not able to go up against the people; for they are stronger than we. Vs 32 And they brought up an evil report of the land which they had searched unto the children of Israel, saying, The land, through which we have gone to search it, is a land that eateth up the inhabitants thereof; and all the people that we saw in it are men of a great stature. Vs 33 And there we saw the giants, the sons of Anak, which come of the giants: and we were in our own sight as grasshoppers, and so we were in their sight.

The result of that direct communication was seen in the very next chapter.

Numbers 14:1 And all the congregation lifted up their voice, and cried; and the people wept that night. Vs 2 And all the children of Israel murmured against Moses and against Aaron: and the whole congregation said unto them, Would God that we had died in the land of Egypt! or would God we had died in this wilderness! Vs 3 And wherefore hath the Lord brought us unto this land, to fall by the sword, that our wives and our children should be a prey? were it not better for us to return into Egypt? Vs 4 And they said one to another, Let us make a captain, and let us return into Egypt.

Unbelief soon spread among the people and they wept that night. Not only did this happen, murmuring spread throughout the camp. Joshua soon sends out spies to check out Jericho.

> **Joshua 2:1** And Joshua the son of Nun sent out of Shittim two men to spy secretly, saying, Go view the land, even Jericho. And they went, and came into an harlot's house, named Rahab, and lodged there… Vs 23 So the two men returned, and descended from the mountain, and passed over, and **came to Joshua the son of Nun, and told him all** things that befell them: Vs 24 And they said unto Joshua, Truly the Lord hath delivered into our hands all the land; for even all the inhabitants of the country do faint because of us.

When they returned from this espionage mission, he speaks with them directly and manages the communication with the people he is to lead.

ELI AND SAMUEL

The account is told of how Hannah received a child of the Lord. She had been without child and had gone to Shiloh. She has an encounter with the prophet Eli.

> **1 Samuel 1:9** So Hannah rose up after they had eaten in Shiloh, and after they had drunk. Now Eli the priest sat upon a seat by a post of the temple of the Lord.Vs 10

And she was in bitterness of soul, and prayed unto the Lord, and wept sore. Vs 11 And she vowed a vow, and said, O Lord of hosts, if thou wilt indeed look on the affliction of thine handmaid, and remember me, and not forget thine handmaid, but wilt give unto thine handmaid a man child, then I will give him unto the Lord all the days of his life, and there shall no razor come upon his head. Vs 12 And it came to pass, as she continued praying before the Lord, that Eli marked her mouth. Vs 13 Now Hannah, she spake in her heart; only her lips moved, but her voice was not heard: therefore Eli thought she had been drunken. Vs 14 And Eli said unto her, How long wilt thou be drunken? put away thy wine from thee. Vs 15 And Hannah answered and said, No, my lord, I am a woman of a sorrowful spirit: I have drunk neither wine nor strong drink, but have poured out my soul before the Lord. Vs 16 Count not thine handmaid for a daughter of Belial: for out of the abundance of my complaint and grief have I spoken hitherto. Vs 17 Then Eli answered and said, Go in peace: and the God of Israel grant thee thy petition that thou hast asked of him. Vs 18 And she said, Let thine handmaid find grace in thy sight. So the woman went her way, and did eat, and her countenance was no more sad. Vs 19 And they rose up in the morning early, and worshipped before the Lord, and returned, and came to their house to Ramah: and Elkanah knew Hannah his wife; and the Lord remembered her. Vs 20 Wherefore it came to pass, when the time was come about after Hannah had conceived, that she bare a son, and called his name Samuel, saying, Because I have asked him of the Lord. Vs 21 And the man Elkanah, and all his house, went up to offer unto the Lord the yearly sacrifice, and his vow. Vs 22 But Hannah went not up; for she said unto her husband, I will not go up until the child be weaned, and then I will bring him, that he may appear before the Lord, and there abide for ever. Vs 23 And Elkanah her husband said unto her, Do what seemeth thee good; tarry until thou have weaned him; only the Lord establish his word. So the woman abode, and gave her son suck until she weaned him. Vs 24 And when she had weaned him, she took him up with her, with three bullocks, and one ephah of flour, and a bottle of wine, and brought him unto the house of the Lord in Shiloh: and the child was young. Vs 25 And they slew a bullock, and brought the child to Eli. Vs 26 And she said, Oh my lord, as thy soul liveth, my lord, I am the woman that stood by thee here, praying unto the Lord. Vs 27 **For this child I prayed; and the Lord hath given me my petition which I asked of him: Vs 28 Therefore also I have lent him to the Lord; as long as he liveth he shall be lent to the Lord.** And he worshipped the Lord there.

By 1 Samuel 3, the child Samuel had become Eli's disciple. A salient truth about missing out on the supernatural because we have been fixated on the spectacular comes to the fore here.

1 Samuel 3:1 And the child Samuel ministered unto the Lord before Eli. And the word of the Lord was precious in those days; there was no open vision. Vs 2 And it came to pass at that time, when Eli was laid down in his place, and his eyes began to wax dim, that he could not see; Vs 3 And ere the lamp of God went out in the temple of the Lord, where the ark of God was, and Samuel was laid down to sleep; Vs 4 That the Lord called Samuel: and he answered, Here am I. Vs 5 And he ran unto Eli, and said, Here am I; for thou calledst me. And he said, I called not; lie down again. And he went and lay down. Vs 6 And the Lord called yet again, Samuel. And Samuel arose and went to Eli, and said, Here am I; for thou didst call me. And he answered, I called not, my son; lie down again. Vs 7 Now Samuel did not yet know the Lord, neither was the word of the Lord yet revealed unto him. Vs 8 And the Lord called Samuel again the third time. And he arose and went to Eli, and said, Here am I; for thou didst call me. And Eli perceived that the Lord had called the child. Vs 9 Therefore Eli said unto Samuel, Go, lie down: and it shall be, if he call thee, that thou shalt say, **Speak, Lord; for thy servant heareth.** So Samuel went and lay down in his place. Vs 10 And the Lord came, and stood, and called as at other times, Samuel, Samuel. Then Samuel answered, **Speak; for thy servant heareth.**

A couple of takeaways:

- Samuel's training was onsite

- Samuel did not yet know the Lord, neither was the word of the Lord yet revealed unto him.
- God used Eli's voice to speak to Samuel
- It took Eli to tell Samuel the Lord was calling him

It reinforces the fact that God's method is man.

The result of that onsite training ended up being a blessing to the whole nation.

> 1 Samuel 3:19 And Samuel grew, and the Lord was with him, and did let none of his words fall to the ground. Vs 20 And all Israel from Dan even to Beersheba knew that Samuel was established to be a prophet of the Lord.

PAUL AND TIMOTHY

Their first meeting is in Acts 16.

> **Acts 16:1** Then came he to Derbe and Lystra: and, behold, a certain disciple was there, named Timotheus, the son of a certain woman, which was a Jewess, and believed; but his father was a Greek: Vs 2 **Which was well reported of by the brethren** that were at Lystra and Iconium. Vs 3 Him would Paul have to go forth with him; and took and circumcised him because of the Jews which were in those quarters: for they knew all that his father was a Greek.

Observe the testimony that he had. He

> **2 Timothy 2:1** Thou therefore, my son, be strong in the grace that is in Christ Jesus. **Vs 2** And **the things that thou hast heard of me** among many witnesses, the same commit thou to faithful men, who shall be able to teach others also.

To Philippi

> **Philippians 2:19** But I trust in the Lord Jesus to send Timotheus shortly unto you, that I also may be of good comfort, when I know your state **Vs 20** For I have no man likeminded, who will naturally care for your state. **Vs 21** For all seek their own, not the things which are Jesus Christ's. **Vs 22** But ye know the proof of him, that, **as a son with the father, he hath served with me in the gospel. Vs 23** Him therefore I hope to send presently, so soon as I shall see how it will go with me.

See his testimony concerning Timothy. As a son with the father, he hath served **WITH ME** in the gospel. It was thus clear that Timothy only taught what Paul taught him. This was further reiterated in 2 Timothy 2 above.

… the things that you have heard of me…

Paul taught. Timothy took notes and taught the same. He is mentioned in all of Paul's letters except Ephesians and Galatians. What an ally.

To underscore the importance and fruit of that personal onsite ministry, he has hands laid on him.

> **1 Timothy 4:14** Neglect not the gift that is in thee, which was given thee by prophecy, with the laying on of the hands of the presbytery. Vs 15 Meditate upon these things; give thyself wholly to them; that thy profiting may appear to all. Vs 16 Take heed unto thyself, and unto the doctrine; continue in them: for in doing this thou shalt both save thyself, and them that hear thee.

> **2 Timothy 1:6** Wherefore I put thee in remembrance that thou stir up the gift of God, which is in thee by the putting on of my hands.

Impartations are a result of this onsite relationship in the local church. To underscore how often this happens when Believers gather, Paul mentions it in his letter to the church in Rome.

> Romans 1:11 For I long to see you, that I may impart unto you some spiritual gift, to the end ye may be established; Vs 12 That is, that I may be comforted together with you by the mutual faith both of you and me.

THE LORD JESUS AND THE APOSTLES

Luke 6:12 And it came to pass in those days, that he went out into a mountain to pray, and continued all night in prayer to God. Vs 13 And when it was day, he called unto him his disciples: and of them he chose twelve, whom also he named apostles; Vs 14 Simon, (whom he also named Peter,) and Andrew his brother, James and John, Philip and Bartholomew, Vs 15 Matthew and Thomas, James the son of Alphaeus, and Simon called Zelotes, Vs 16 And Judas the brother of James, and Judas Iscariot, which also was the traitor. Vs 17 And he came down with them, and stood in the plain, and the company of his disciples, and a great multitude of people out of all Judaea and Jerusalem, and from the sea coast of Tyre and Sidon, which came to hear him, and to be healed of their diseases;

His choosing of his disciples is preceded by all-night praying. Observe what he does next. He called unto him his disciples. This was clearly a physical gathering. Same thing in Matthew 4. This happened after the baptism of John in Matthew 3.

Matthew 4:1 Then was Jesus led up of the Spirit into the wilderness to be tempted of the devil… **Vs 17** From that time Jesus began to preach, and to say, Repent: for the kingdom of heaven is at hand. **Vs 18** And Jesus, walking by the sea of Galilee, **saw two brethren, Simon called Peter, and Andrew his brother, casting a net**

into the sea: for they were fishers. **Vs 19 And he saith unto them, Follow me, and I will make you fishers of men. Vs 20 And they straightway left their nets, and followed him. Vs 21 And going on from thence, he saw other two brethren, James the son of Zebedee, and John his brother, in a ship with Zebedee their father, mending their nets; and he called them. Vs 22 And they immediately left the ship and their father, and followed him.**

Observe the sequence. He saw them. He called them. This clearly happened onsite. The Lord Jesus was known to have a custom that honoured physical gatherings.

Luke 2:42 And when he was twelve years old, they went up to Jerusalem after the custom of the feast. Vs 43 And when they had fulfilled the days, as they returned, the child Jesus tarried behind in Jerusalem; and Joseph and his mother knew not of it. Vs 44 But they, supposing him to have been in the company, went a day's journey; and they sought him among their kinsfolk and acquaintance. Vs 45 And when they found him not, they turned back again to Jerusalem, seeking him. **Vs 46 And it came to pass, that after three days they found him in the temple, sitting in the midst of the doctors, both hearing them, and asking them questions.** Vs 47 And all that heard him were astonished at his understanding and answers. Vs 48 And when they saw him, they were amazed: and his mother said unto him, Son, why hast thou thus dealt with us? behold, thy father and I have sought thee sorrowing. Vs 49 And he said unto them, How is it that ye sought me? wist ye not that I must be about my Father's business? Vs 50 And they understood not the saying which he spake unto them. Vs 51 And he went down with them, and came to Nazareth, and was subject unto them: but his mother kept all these sayings in her heart.

Luke provides this account as a precursor to how he would describe Jesus' ministry much later.

Luke 4:14 And Jesus returned in the power of the Spirit into Galilee: and there went out a fame of him through all the region round about. **Vs 15 And he taught in their synagogues,** being glorified of all. Vs 16 And he came to Nazareth, where he had been brought up: **and, as his custom was, he went into the synagogue on the sabbath day, and stood up for to read**. **Vs 17** And there was delivered unto him the book of the prophet Esaias. And when he had opened the book, he found the place where it was written, **Vs 18** The Spirit of the Lord is upon me, because he hath anointed me to preach the gospel to the poor; he hath sent me to heal the brokenhearted, to preach deliverance to the captives, and recovering of sight to the blind, to set at liberty them that are bruised, Vs 19 To preach the acceptable year of the Lord. Vs 20 And he closed the book, and he gave it again to the minister, and sat down. And the eyes of all them that were in the synagogue were fastened on him. Vs 21 And he began to say unto them, This day is this scripture fulfilled in your ears.

Notice that emphasis in verse 16- as his custom was. A custom refers to that which you are known for. It refers to something that you do all the time. Jesus prized physical gatherings so much so that it was used to describe his earthly ministry.

Acts 10:36 The word which God sent unto the children of Israel, preaching peace by Jesus Christ: (he is Lord of all:) Vs 37 That word, I say, ye know, which was published throughout all Judaea, and began from Galilee, **after the baptism which John preached;** Vs 38 How God anointed Jesus of Nazareth with the Holy Ghost and with power: who went about doing good, and healing all that were oppressed of the devil; for God was with him.

After the baptism which John preached. This undoubtedly refers to Jesus' announcement to Israel at the Jordan. This was definitely a watershed moment in his ministry as it does get a mention when Judas is to be replaced.

Acts 1:15 And in those days Peter stood up in the midst of the disciples, and said, (the number of names together were about an hundred and twenty,) Vs 16 Men and brethren, this scripture must needs have been fulfilled, which the Holy Ghost by the mouth of David spake before concerning Judas, which was guide to

> them that took Jesus. Vs 17 For he was numbered with us, and had obtained part of this ministry. Vs 18 Now this man purchased a field with the reward of iniquity; and falling headlong, he burst asunder in the midst, and all his bowels gushed out. Vs 19 And it was known unto all the dwellers at Jerusalem; insomuch as that field is called in their proper tongue, Aceldama, that is to say, The field of blood. Vs 20 For it is written in the book of Psalms, Let his habitation be desolate, and let no man dwell therein: and his bishoprick let another take. **Vs 21 Wherefore of these men which have companied with us all the time that the Lord Jesus went in and out among us, Vs 22 Beginning from the baptism of John,** unto that same day that he was taken up from us, must one be ordained to be a witness with us of his resurrection. Vs 23 And they appointed two, Joseph called Barsabas, who was surnamed Justus, and Matthias. Vs 24 And they prayed, and said, Thou, Lord, which knowest the hearts of all men, shew whether of these two thou hast chosen, Vs 25 That he may take part of this ministry and apostleship, from which Judas by transgression fell, that he might go to his own place. Vs 26 And they gave forth their lots; and the lot fell upon Matthias; and he was numbered with the eleven apostles.

There were watershed moments and meetings in Jesus' ministry. One of those was the baptism of John. Observe a very important detail (as earlier explained) in verse 21-

> Vs 21 Wherefore of these men **which have companied with us all the time** that the Lord Jesus went in and out among us,

One key metric that was used to determine Judas' replacement was one who had companied with them all the time. He had to be a person who had companied with them all the time. Hence, he had to be someone who was physically present and went about with Jesus as he ministered all around the nation.

The Book of Acts is filled with accounts of Believers gathering together. Thus, it was the Book that captured how the apostles practiced and carried out the instructions that the Lord gave. Before we proceed, observe a key detail in Mark 3.

> **Mark 3:14** And he ordained twelve, **that they should be with him**, and that he might send them forth to preach, Vs 15 And to have power to heal sicknesses, and to cast out devils:

Jesus called them that they should be with him (physically).

Therefore, we can say very clearly, that gathering together is at the heart of Christian service. Whilst we are thankful for technology, the believer is required to ensure that they do not replace the instructions to gather together as seen, taught and practiced through the scriptures. While technology in its various forms have helped in advancing the course, it must not be used to replace or review

Christian gatherings. While meetings are recorded and can be stored and transmitted in digital formats, God's unchanging plan as seen in his word yet requires that we gather. When a believer watches a service of believers gathered together, what they have done is watch other believers gather. It is a slippery slope that we must be extremely mindful of and careful of. The local church is not therefore to be described under any guise or format as an online church, to think otherwise is to become secular or non-biblical in our worldview. It is to also side-step clear scriptural instructions and thereby lose out on the blessedness of physical gatherings such as diverse impartations, particularly through the ministry of the laying on of hands. The local church is not an online church, or a place for comedy and/or entertainment, nor is it an empowerment or skills acquisition centre. It is also not a Whatsapp, Twitter (X), Facebook or whatever social media platform made available by today's technology to give room to bible study groups with no accountability or submission to defined church leaders or authority.

CHAPTER 3

ROLE OF THE LOCAL CHURCH

As earlier explained in the previous chapters, the local church is a physical gathering of believers in a particular location, with a particular leadership (Pastor), who leads and trains the believers with the teaching of the scriptures. The local church is the centre point of spiritual growth and pivotal to the effectiveness of the believers in the plan of God for the earth. As earlier mentioned, the local church is a specific place where believers gather to be taught, trained, and modelled after Christ. The believers in turn have a responsibility to be obedient, submissive, and accountable to the leadership of the local church that he belongs.

Hence, a primary role of the local church is to raise disciples.

Discipleship

Matthew 28:18 And Jesus came and spake unto them, saying, All power is given unto me in heaven and in earth. Vs 19 Go ye therefore, and teach all nations, baptizing them in the name of the Father, and of the Son, and of the Holy Ghost: Vs 20 Teaching them to observe all things whatsoever I have commanded you: and, lo, I am with you alway, even unto the end of the world. Amen.

It is important to know that the authors of the New Testament books wrote from the writings of the Old Testament, hence Jesus in this text must have taken this instruction from the writings of the Old Testament authors. Let us consider such texts:

Exodus 18:12 And Jethro, Moses' father in law, took a burnt offering and sacrifices for God: and Aaron came, and all the elders of Israel, to eat bread with Moses' father in law before God. 18:13 And it came to pass on the morrow, that Moses sat to judge the people: and the people stood by Moses from the morning unto the evening. 18:14 And when Moses' father in law saw all that he did to the people, he said, What is this thing that thou doest to the people? why sittest thou thyself alone, and all the people stand by thee from morning unto even? 18:15 And Moses said unto his father in law, Because the people come unto me to enquire of God: 18:16 When they have a matter, they come unto me; and

I judge between one and another, and I do make them know the statutes of God, and his laws. 18:17 And Moses' father in law said unto him, The thing that thou doest is not good. 18:18 Thou wilt surely wear away, both thou, and this people that is with thee: for this thing is too heavy for thee; thou art not able to perform it thyself alone. 18:19 Hearken now unto my voice, I will give thee counsel, and God shall be with thee: Be thou for the people to God-ward, that thou mayest bring the causes unto God: 18:20 And thou shalt teach them ordinances and laws, and shalt shew them the way wherein they must walk, and the work that they must do. 18:21 Moreover thou shalt provide out of all the people able men, such as fear God, men of truth, hating covetousness; and place such over them, to be rulers of thousands, and rulers of hundreds, rulers of fifties, and rulers of tens: 18:22 And let them judge the people at all seasons: and it shall be, that every great matter they shall bring unto thee, but every small matter they shall judge: so shall it be easier for thyself, and they shall bear the burden with thee.

Jethro, Moses' father-in-law recommends that Moses appoint qualified men to handle judgement, including teaching and instructing others. This counsel emphasises the art of delegating the teaching responsibility to others in order to reach more people and make oversight more effective.

Hence, Jesus must have taken a cue from this and applied the same instructing his disciples to go and make disciples of all nations via teaching.

> **Matthew 28:18** And Jesus came and spake unto them, saying, All power is given unto me in heaven and in earth. **Vs 19** Go ye therefore, and **teach** all nations, baptizing them in the name of the Father, and of the Son, and of the Holy Ghost: **Vs 20 Teaching** them to observe all things whatsoever I have commanded you: and, lo, I am with you alway, even unto the end of the world. Amen.

The word "**teach**" in vs 19 was translated from the Greek word "**matheteuo,**" it implies to make disciples. It was derived from another Greek word "**mathetes**" which implies a student, one who is learning, a disciple. The word "**Teaching**" in **verse 20** was translated from the Greek word "**didasko,**" it implies to expound, to explain. It is vital to note that the word "**didasko**" was used many times in relation to Jesus in the synoptics.

Therefore, the apostles were commanded by Jesus to make disciples of every nation, this will be done primarily by teaching them. This is local church in view. So the Apostles' doctrine is the doctrine of Christ and that is the tool for discipleship.

The word "make disciples" implies to train people on how to think, talk and act. This refers to their conduct being changed by teaching.

"**Disciple**" is someone who takes information and instructions (training). The apostles heeding to the instructions of Jesus went ahead to make disciples, hence we the use of this word in the book of Acts of Apostles.

> **Acts 2:41** Then they that gladly received his word were baptized: and the same day there were added *unto them* about three thousand souls. **Vs42** And **they continued stedfastly** in the apostles' doctrine and fellowship, and in breaking of bread, and in prayers.

...they that gladly received his word ...they continued steadfastly.

> **Acts 2:44** And all that believed were together, and had all things common;

Notice that they are gathering in one place under a particular leadership of the Apostles.

What were they doing?

> **Vs. 42** And **they continued stedfastly** in the apostles' doctrine and fellowship

The word **"Doctrine"** was translated from the Greek word " **didache**" It refers to instruction (the act or the matter): hath been taught. it is from the Greek word " **Didasko"** which implies teaching. This will imply the teaching itself and the way it is communicated.

All through the book of Acts, the use of the word 'Disciple(s)' was prominent as the apostles were involved in training the believers as Jesus did to them and instructed them to do the same.

Let us consider the texts where this word was used.

> Acts 1:15 And in those days Peter stood up in the midst of the disciples, and said, (the number of names together were about an hundred and twenty,)
>
> Acts 6:1 And in those days, when the number of the disciples was multiplied, there arose a murmuring of the Grecians against the Hebrews, because their widows were neglected in the daily ministration. Acts 6:2 Then the twelve called the multitude of the disciples unto them, and said, It is not reason that we should leave the word of God, and serve tables.
>
> Acts 6:7 And the word of God increased; and the number of the disciples multiplied in Jerusalem greatly; and a great company of the priests were obedient to the faith.
>
> Acts 9:1 And Saul, yet breathing out threatenings and slaughter against the disciples of the Lord, went unto the high priest,
>
> Acts 9:10 And there was a certain disciple at Damascus, named Ananias; and to him said the Lord in a vision, Ananias. And he said, Behold, I am here, Lord.

Acts 9:19 And when he had received meat, he was strengthened. Then was Saul certain days with the disciples which were at Damascus.

Acts 9:25 Then the disciples took him by night, and let him down by the wall in a basket. Acts 9:26 And when Saul was come to Jerusalem, he assayed to join himself to the disciples: but they were all afraid of him, and believed not that he was a disciple.

Acts 9:36 Now there was at Joppa a certain disciple named Tabitha, which by interpretation is called Dorcas: this woman was full of good works and almsdeeds which she did.

Acts 9:38 And forasmuch as Lydda was nigh to Joppa, and the disciples had heard that Peter was there, they sent unto him two men, desiring him that he would not delay to come to them.

Acts 11:26 And when he had found him, he brought him unto Antioch. And it came to pass, that a whole year they assembled themselves with the church, and taught much people. And the disciples were called Christians first in Antioch.

Acts 11:29 Then the disciples, every man according to his ability, determined to send relief unto the brethren which dwelt in Judaea:

Acts 13:52 And the disciples were filled with joy, and with the Holy Ghost.

Acts 14:20 Howbeit, as the disciples stood round about him, he rose up, and came into the city: and the next day he departed with Barnabas to Derbe.

Acts 14:22 Confirming the souls of the disciples, and exhorting them to continue in the faith, and that we must through much tribulation enter into the kingdom of God.

Acts 14:28 And there they abode long time with the disciples.

Acts 15:10 Now therefore why tempt ye God, to put a yoke upon the neck of the disciples, which neither our fathers nor we were able to bear?

Acts 16:1 Then came he to Derbe and Lystra: and, behold, a certain disciple was there, named Timotheus, the son of a certain woman, which was a Jewess, and believed; but his father was a Greek:

Acts 18:23 And after he had spent some time there, he departed, and went over all the country of Galatia and Phrygia in order, strengthening all the disciples.

Acts 18:27 And when he was disposed to pass into Achaia, the brethren wrote, exhorting the disciples to receive him: who, when he was come, helped them much which had believed through grace:

Acts 19:1 And it came to pass, that, while Apollos was at Corinth, Paul having passed through the upper coasts came to Ephesus: and finding certain disciples,

Acts 19:9 But when divers were hardened, and believed not, but spake evil of that way before the multitude, he departed from them, and separated the disciples, disputing daily in the school of one Tyrannus.

Acts 19:30 And when Paul would have entered in unto the people, the disciples suffered him not.

Acts 20:1 And after the uproar was ceased, Paul called unto him the disciples, and embraced them, and departed for to go into Macedonia.

Acts 20:7 And upon the first day of the week, when the disciples came together to break bread, Paul preached unto them, ready to depart on the morrow; and continued his speech until midnight.

Acts 20:30 Also of your own selves shall men arise, speaking perverse things, to draw away disciples after them.

Acts 21:4 And finding disciples, we tarried there seven days: who said to Paul through the Spirit, that he should not go up to Jerusalem.

Acts 21:16 There went with us also certain of the disciples of Caesarea, and brought with them one Mnason of Cyprus, an old disciple, with whom we should lodge.

The above texts showed that raising disciples is a major role of the local church in the lives of the believers.

That same information that makes you a disciple is what you are being trained with (the Gospel).

2 Timothy 2:2 And the things that thou hast heard of me among many witnesses, the same commit thou to faithful men, who shall be able to teach others also.

The local church trains the believer into being a disciple, where he receives the training from his Pastor and passes the same to others.

Observe where the word **"doctrine" (teaching)** was written in the following texts of the scriptures.

Titus 1: 9 Holding fast the faithful word as he hath been taught, that he may be able by sound doctrine both to exhort and to convince the gainsayers.

2 Timothy 3:14 But **continue** thou in the things which thou hast learned and hast been assured of, knowing of whom thou hast learned them; Vs 15 And that from **a child** thou hast known the holy scriptures, which are able to make thee wise unto salvation through faith which is in Christ Jesus. Vs 16 All scripture is given by inspiration of God, and is profitable for doctrine, for reproof, for correction, for instruction in righteousness: Vs 17 That **the man of God** may be perfect, t**horoughly furnished unto all good works**.

The profitability of the scriptures is in teaching it.

1 Timothy 4:16 Take heed unto thyself, and unto the doctrine; continue in them: for in doing this thou shalt both save thyself, and them that hear thee.

1st Timothy 5:17 Let the elders that rule well be counted worthy of double honour, especially they who labour in the word and doctrine.

Ephesians 4:14 That we *henceforth* be no more children, tossed to and fro, and carried about with every wind of doctrine, by the sleight of men, *and* cunning craftiness, whereby they lie in wait to deceive; Vs 15 But speaking the truth in love, may grow up into him in all things, which is the head, *even* Christ

2nd John 1:7 For many deceivers are entered into the world, who confess not that Jesus Christ is come in the flesh. This is a deceiver and an antichrist. **Vs 8** Look to yourselves, that we lose not those things which we have wrought, but that we receive a full reward. **Vs 9** Whosoever transgresseth, and abideth not in the doctrine of Christ, hath not God. He that abideth in the doctrine of Christ, he hath both the Father and the Son.

Vs 10 If there come any unto you, **and bring not this doctrine**, receive him not into *your* house, neither bid him God speed: **Vs 11** For he that biddeth him God speed is partaker of his evil deeds.

The local church is central to discipleship. This is achieved by teaching, explanation of the scriptures and then corrections and instructions. Knowledge is thus very vital to the believer. That knowledge is made available in the local church through men and women that God has made available (Pastors).

The local church is where the believer grows up spiritually;

Ephesians 4:11 And he gave some, apostles; and some, prophets; and some, evangelists; and some, pastors and teachers; **Vs12** For the perfecting of the saints, for the work of the ministry, for the edifying of the body of Christ: **Vs13** Till we all come in the unity of the faith, and of the knowledge of the Son of God, unto a perfect man, unto the measure of the stature of the fulness of Christ: **Vs 14** That we *henceforth* be no more children, tossed to and fro, and carried about with every wind of doctrine, by the sleight of men, *and* cunning craftiness, whereby they lie in wait to deceive; **Vs15** But speaking the truth in love, may grow up into him in all things, which is the head, *even* Christ: **Vs16** From whom the whole body fitly joined together and compacted by that which every joint supplieth, according to the effectual working in the measure of every part, maketh increase of the body unto the edifying of itself in love.

Apostles, prophets, evangelists, pastors in the local church all have a singular purpose and function: it is to mature the saints. That is spiritual growth.

The word **"for"** in the text above was translated from the Greek word "PROS" which implies "in view of". The word "**perfecting"** was translated from the Greek word "KATARTISMOS" which implies to equip, to fit things properly and in this context, for the work of Ministry.

So, the Pastor is to mature believers "**in view of"** making them fit properly for the work of Ministry. He gave gifts to men, in view of fitting saints in their proper place in the work of ministry. He was talking about the function of the leadership of the local church.

Ephesians 4:13 Till we all come in the unity of the faith, and of the knowledge of the Son of God, unto a perfect man, unto the measure of the stature of the fulness of Christ:

... 'Till we all come' is used for arriving at a goal. It is the Greek word "**katantao"** - it means to reach a goal.

What is that goal or the essence of Pastoring?

To attain to the unity of the faith, that is; the knowledge of the Son of God. It doesn't refer to different church denominations coming together. "We all" implies we individually arrive at this destination. That is, God expects that all believers should grow up spiritually.

Let's further examine the word **"till we all come".** Paul used the same word in **Philippians 3**

> **Philippians 3:11** If by any means I might attain unto the resurrection of the dead. **Vs 12** Not as though I had already attained, either were already perfect: but I follow after, if that I may apprehend that for which also I am apprehended of Christ Jesus.

To attain is the same word **"till we all come";** it always refers to the end of a journey. That is, this is where we are going; this is what it is. All believers are expected to foster their growth and maturity under their pastors' oversight. This maturity is achieved when we collectively reach a unity of the faith.

The word 'unity of the faith' was used in Ephesians 4:3.

> **Ephesians 4:3** Endeavouring to keep the unity of the Spirit in the bond of peace.

Referring to agreement. What is that agreement?

That is, two things must come together. The believer is coming into agreement with the faith. He is to mature to come to the end point--the unity of the faith. That maturity/understanding is in the mind, via teaching.

Ephesians 4:13 Till we all come in the unity of the faith, and of the **knowledge** of the Son of God, unto a perfect man, unto the measure of the stature of the fulness of Christ:

The word "knowledge" was translated from the Greek word **"epignosis".**

Gnosis is knowledge. **"epignosis"** is full knowledge. The knowledge of the son of God is what counts for maturity.

The word knowledge was translated from the Greek word "epignosis". It was written in: **Philemon 1:6.**

Philemon 1:6 That the communication of thy faith may become effectual by the acknowledging of every good thing which is in you in Christ Jesus.

The word acknowledging was translated from the same word **"epignosis"** which implies: Precise, comprehension / understanding of what is yours in Christ.

Peter affirms:

1st Peter 2:2 As newborn babes, desire the sincere milk of the word, that ye may grow thereby:

The word 'sincere' has to do with thinking. Some versions have 'mental milk'. You grow in your insight.

2 Peter 3:18 But grow in grace, and *in* the knowledge of our Lord and Saviour Jesus Christ. To him *be* glory both now and for ever. Amen.

When the believer starts to know who Jesus is, he comes to an agreement of that knowledge. That agreement starts with his thinking. The knowledge of the son of God; the measure of the stature of the fullness of Christ.

There is no growth without knowledge. Growth is based on insight. Service will flow from that. We have a measure. A believer then begins to think and see Jesus as his saviour. He begins to mature in thinking. We do not have full knowledge of the son at salvation. From receiving salvation, the believer begins to align his thinking consistently with full knowledge. Salvation started with knowledge and hence, the believer should continue growing in knowledge.

Ephesians 4: 14 **"Children"** here is NEPIOS which means an undeveloped infant.

Ephesians 4:15 But speaking the truth in love, may grow up into him in all things, which is the head, *even* Christ: **Vs16** From whom the whole body fitly joined together and compacted by that which every joint supplieth, according to the effectual working in the measure of every part, maketh increase of the body unto the edifying of itself in love.

Vs 15-16 Everything Paul mentions here is for the church. So, therefore, they are local church based.

Colossians 1:27 To whom God would make known what is the riches of the glory of this mystery among the Gentiles; which is Christ in you, the hope of glory: **Vs 28** Whom we preach, warning every man, and teaching every man in all wisdom; that we may present every man perfect in Christ Jesus:

The pastors are expected to present every man perfect **(MARTURE)** in Christ Jesus. Pastors have the responsibility to mature believers. Being a pastor is not a title but a function which is defined by your labour over the flock committed to you in your local assembly

1 Thessalonians 5:12 And we beseech you, brethren, to know them **which labour among you**, and are over you in the Lord, and admonish you;

Observe the term '**which labour among you**.' This refers to a definite location. They are among you and are over you in the Lord. This refers to the local church

1 Thessalonians 5:13 And to esteem them very highly in love for their work's sake. And be at peace among yourselves. **Vs 14** Now we exhort you, brethren, warn them that are unruly, comfort the feebleminded, support the weak, be patient toward all men.

There are definite men and women that are recognized who are over you in the Lord. This is found in the local church.

> **Hebrews 13:17** Obey them that have the rule over you, and submit yourselves: for they watch for your souls, as they that must give account, that they may do it with joy, and not with grief: for that is unprofitable for you.

The word 'rule' there refers to control. These are people that give account of your life, and they are found in the local church.

Spiritual growth is when you are growing in insight concerning Christ.

> **Matthew 28:19**Go ye therefore, and teach all nations, baptizing them in the name of the Father, and of the Son, and of the Holy Ghost **Vs 20** Teaching them to observe all things whatsoever I have commanded you: and, lo, I am with you alway, *even* unto the end of the world. Amen.

...Teaching them to observe all things whatsoever I have commanded you:

That same information that makes you a disciple is what you are being trained with.

2 Timothy 2:2 And the things that thou hast heard of me among many witnesses, the same commit thou to faithful men, who shall be able to teach others also.

The church is a place where you keep teaching. We keep giving out information.

Hence, the phrase "till we all come in the unity of the faith" in Ephesians 4:13, refers to each believer/disciple coming to maturity via the knowledge (of Christ) communicated in the Local Church, by the Pastor or leaders.

Therefore, for the believer to grow spiritually, he or she must be fed with the knowledge of the son of God (the reality of every good thing in him, in Christ.)

In Verse 20, he described it as the learning of Christ!

Ephesians 4:20 But ye have not so learned Christ; **Vs 21** If so be that ye have heard him, and have been taught by him, as the truth is in Jesus:

Thus, when a believer is growing spiritually, he is stable on God's word. His assurance is formed from the written word all that God has done in Christ, and not experiences, visions, opinions, and hearsay.

Accountability and submission

Accountability and submission in the context of the local church is to protect the members by having their lives under control. This brings about caution to them. It is thus important to know how to recognise the leaders in the local church such that the believer would know who to submit and be accountable to. The epistles speak in clear terms of who these leaders are. They are those saddled with the responsibility of preaching, teaching and exercising oversight function. The following scriptures lend credence to this.

> **1 Thessalonians 5:12** And we beseech you, brethren, to know them which labour among you, and are over you in the Lord, and admonish you; 5:13 And to esteem them very highly in love for their work's sake. And be at peace among yourselves.

> **1 Timothy 5:17** Let the elders that rule well be counted worthy of double honour, especially they who labour in the word and doctrine.

> **Hebrews 13:7** Remember them which have the rule over you, who have spoken unto you the word of God: whose faith follow, considering the end of their conversation.

The leaders guide and members willingly submit, the scripture emphasises the importance of obedience to church leaders.

Hebrews 13:17 Obey them that have the rule over you, and submit yourselves: for they watch for your souls, as they that must give account, that they may do it with joy, and not with grief: for that is unprofitable for you.

This verse highlights the dual responsibility of leaders to guide members to submit willingly. Leaders are to watch over the souls of the members, and they will give an account to God for their lives. Members, in turn, are encouraged to obey and submit, recognizing the leaders' accountability to God.

This shows that the church operates within God's system of caution and control, as seen in Jesus' cautioning of his disciples.

Matthew 16:6 Then Jesus said unto them, Take heed and beware of the leaven of the Pharisees and of the Sadducees.

Jesus used the metaphor of leaven to caution his disciples about the teachings and influence of the religious leaders (Pharisees and Sadducees). He warned against adopting their hypocritical and legalistic attitudes, emphasizing the need for true and sincere worship of God.

Matthew 26:41 Watch and pray, that ye enter not into temptation: the spirit indeed is willing, but the flesh is weak.

In the Garden of Gethsemane, Jesus urged his disciples to be vigilant and prayerful, knowing the human vulnerability to yield to temptation. This admonition highlights the importance of relying on the power of prayer in the face of challenges.

> **Matthew 24:4** And Jesus answered and said unto them, Take heed that no man deceive you

Jesus emphasised the prevalence of deception. He warned them to be discerning and not easily carried away by false teachings, emphasising the necessity of staying true to his teachings.

> **Luke 12:15** And he said unto them, Take heed, and beware of covetousness: for a man's life consisteth not in the abundance of the things which he possesseth.

Jesus cautioned against the pitfalls of greed and materialism, emphasizing that true life is not measured by wealth. This teaching encourages disciples to prioritise spiritual growth over the pursuit of worldly possessions.

The church becomes a place where individuals willingly submit to authority for their spiritual well-being, creating a culture of control that aligns with biblical teachings. We also see such caution in the epistles;

> 1 Corinthians 10:12 Wherefore let him that thinketh he standeth take heed lest he fall.

Paul urges the Corinthians to avoid pride. The phrase "let him that thinketh he standeth take heed lest he fall" serves as a caution against arrogance, emphasizing the importance of humility and the awareness of one's vulnerability to temptation.

Colossians 2:8 Beware lest any man spoil you through philosophy and vain deceit, after the tradition of men, after the rudiments of the world, and not after Christ.

Paul warns the Colossians to be wary of deceptive philosophies that may divert them from the true teachings of Christ. "Beware lest any man spoil you through philosophy and vain deceit" emphasises the need for discernment, urging believers to anchor their faith in Christ rather than being influenced by worldly ideologies.

1 Timothy 4:16 Take heed unto thyself, and unto the doctrine; continue in them: for in doing this thou shalt both save thyself, and them that hear thee.

Paul instructs Timothy to be vigilant about his walk as a believer and ensuring the soundness of his teachings. "Take heed unto thyself, and unto the doctrine" stresses the dual responsibility of personal conduct and doctrinal fidelity.

2 Peter 3:17 Ye therefore, beloved, seeing ye know these things before, beware lest ye also, being led away with the error of the wicked, fall from your own stedfastness.

Peter cautions the beloved, reminding them to remain steadfast and avoid being led astray by the errors of the wicked. "Beware lest ye also, being led away with the error of the wicked, fall from your own steadfastness" underscores the need for believers to guard against external influences that may compromise their spiritual stability, emphasizing the value of unwavering commitment to the faith.

Conflict resolution in and Outside the Local Church

Conflict resolution is one of the issues handled in the local assembly. The potential for conflict exists where two or more people are present, and the local church is the gathering of people in a specific place. People often experience conflict as a result of divergent ideas and opinions, conflicting ambitions and goals, and varying needs and concerns. The potential for conflict is never far away. It crouches at the door ready to move in to disrupt and divide.

The church must ever be prepared to handle conflict whenever it arises.

Conflict that is dealt with, discussed, managed, and resolved can be good because it provides an opportunity for growth and change. On the other hand, conflict that is left unattended and ignored can destroy unity, hinder growth, and render ministry ineffective.

This was what James pointed out in his epistles:

> **James 4**:1 From whence *come* wars and fightings among you? *come they* not hence, *even* of your lusts that war in your members? **Vs. 2** Ye lust, and have not: ye kill, and desire to have, and cannot obtain: ye fight and war, yet ye have not, because ye ask not.

The word "**lust**" was translated from the Greek word "**hedone**" From handanō (to please); sensual delight; desire, pleasure.

James points to self-centred desire as a source of conflict. He refers to "your desires" (verse 1); "You want something"; "You kill and covet" (verse 2); Notice how often the words "you" and "your" appear. Church conflict occurs when people in the congregation put their personal ideas, thoughts, and motives above what is best for the congregation. The local church is to destroy that selfishness and when this is not yet achieved it result in conflict.

Another source of church conflict pointed out by James is anger or hate. The hallmark of the church and its most perfect means of ministering to the world is love. Yet James tells us that Christians are capable of killing (figuratively speaking) one another with hate. When a Christian manifest a hateful attitude toward another Christian it is misplaced anger. Oftentimes, church conflict is the result of some angry person looking for scapegoat to vent on. Often the church, the pastor, or someone else becomes the recipient of transferred aggression.

> **Matthew 18:7** Woe unto the world because of offences! for it must needs be that offences come; but woe to that man by whom the offence cometh!

> **Luke 17:1** Then said he unto the disciples, It is impossible but that offences will come: but woe unto him, through whom they come!

Hence, as long as there exists human interactions, there will be reasons to get offended, if not properly attended to.

Likewise, in the local Church, being an assembly of different kinds of believers, reasons to be offended will arise which will cause strife and division if not handled scripturally. The love of God is God's wisdom in our relationships.

How we handle offences many times determine our longevity in a local Church, because offenses not handled with the wisdom of God lead to strife and division. The word "offence" implies a trap, a snare, a stumbling block. That is, in a local Church; traps, snares, stumbling blocks are sure to come. Offences will come from fellow believers and even Church leadership, but our response must always be God's word.

The church is the place of God's authority in the earth. The church is where we make decisions. Hence our decision is different from that of the world.

How do we Handle Conflict When it Arises?

Let's observe what Jesus said about conflict resolution.

> **Matthew 18:15** Moreover if thy brother shall trespass against thee, go and tell him his fault between thee and him alone: if he shall hear thee, thou hast gained thy brother. **Vs 16** But if he will not hear *thee, then* take with thee one or two more, that in the mouth of two or three witnesses every word may be established. **Vs 17 And if he shall neglect to hear them, tell *it* unto the church: but if he neglect to hear the church, let him be unto thee as an heathen man and a publican.** **Vs 18** Verily I say unto you, Whatsoever ye shall bind on earth shall be bound in heaven: and whatsoever ye shall loose on earth shall be loosed in heaven. **Vs 19** Again I say unto you, That if two of you shall agree on earth as touching any thing that they shall ask, it shall be done for them of my Father which is in heaven. **Vs 20** For where two or three are gathered together in my name, there am I in the midst of them. **Vs 21** Then came Peter to him, and said, Lord, how oft shall my brother sin against me, and I forgive him? till seven times? **Vs 22** Jesus saith unto

him, I say not unto thee, Until seven times: but, Until seventy times seven.

Observe what Jesus said: if your brother trespass against you

1st step - Go and meet him personally.

2nd step – If he does not hear you, take one or two people to meet him.

3rd step - If he does not accept, you tell the church.

Notice that the subject of discussion was forgiveness. Jesus was discussing forgiveness. As a believer you must explore every opportunity to gain your brother.

...Go to him first...

Jesus teaches active forgiveness. You are the initiator of the action. This action cannot be carried out without speaking to or with the person. You do not exhaust the options for reconciliation.

Would you have treated the fellow the same way if he was your natural family member?

> **Matthew 18:18** Verily I say unto you, **Whatsoever** ye shall **bind** on earth shall be bound in heaven: and whatsoever ye shall loose on earth shall be loosed in heaven.

The word "**bind**" was translated from the Greek word "**deo**" which was used severally in the New Testament Greek. It has three applications:

1. To declare something as unlawful
2. To literally tie someone with a rope
3. To restrict or to compel

How were these three applied?

Matthew 16:19 And I will give unto thee the keys of the kingdom of heaven: and whatsoever thou shalt bind on earth shall be bound in heaven: and **whatsoever** thou shalt loose on earth shall be loosed in heaven.

Observe that Jesus uses '**whatsoever**' and not '**whosoever**' because he is not referring to persons or demons. He was referring to activities, events or occurrences.

Let us see other texts where the word "bind" or "bound" is applied.

Matthew 12:29 Or else how can one enter into a strong man's house, and spoil his goods, except he first **bind** the strong man? and then he will spoil his house.

The word "**bind**" in this text is to restrict the strong man.

The account in Acts 20 is very vital.

Acts 20:21 Testifying both to the Jews, and also to the Greeks, repentance toward God, and faith toward our

Lord Jesus Christ. **Vs 22** And now, behold, I go **bound** in the spirit unto Jerusalem, not knowing the things that shall befall me there:

That he was bound in the spirit means that he was compelled to go to Jerusalem, and nothing would hold him back.

Romans 7:2 For the **woman which hath an husband is bound by the law** to her husband so long as he liveth; but if the husband be dead, she is loosed from the law of her husband.

1 Corinthians 7:27 Art thou **bound** unto a wife? seek not to be loosed. Art thou **loosed** from a wife? seek not a wife.

Paul was discussing marriage in the text above and uses the terms '**bound**' and '**loosed**'

1 Corinthians 7:39 The wife is **bound by the law** as long as her husband liveth; but if her husband be dead, she is at liberty to be married to whom she will; only in the Lord.

In other words, binding implies an obligation to act. Whatever you bind is something you have an obligation towards, you decide to act on, bind yourself to. Hence, the usage of the word "**bind**" in Matthew 18 is in the context of activities that are either permitted or disallowed.

The word "**loose**" was translated from the Greek word "**luo**" and it means to release or to annul. It is similar to the word translated as "**broken down**" in Ephesians 2:14 where it is used for sin.

> **Ephesians 2:14** For he is our peace, who hath made both one, and hath **broken down** the middle wall of partition between us;

Recall that binding deals with activities, and not people or beings.

> **Matthew 18:22** Jesus saith unto him, I say not unto thee, Until seven times: but, **Until seventy times seven.**

The believer is obligated to forgive 490 times in one day. That clearly is a play of words to show that there is no limit to how often one must exercise forgiveness. And if you should go to him with two or three witnesses, that means you will need a minimum of 980 believers to reconcile with a single brother.

Furthermore;

> **Luke 17:1** Then said he unto the disciples, It is impossible but that offences will come: but woe unto him, through whom they come! **Vs 2** It were better for him that a millstone were hanged about his neck, and he cast into the sea, than that he should offend one of these little ones. **Vs 3** Take heed to yourselves: If thy brother trespass against thee, rebuke him; and if he

repent, forgive him. **Vs 4** And if he trespass against thee seven times in a day, and seven times in a day **turn again** to thee, saying, I repent; thou shalt forgive him. **Vs 5** And the apostles said unto the Lord, Increase our faith.

The phrase "**turn again**" in verse 4 was translated from the Greek word, "**epistrepho,**" which implies to turn around, to repent.

Note that the usage of the phrase '**in a day**' does not imply a 24-hour cycle of time, instead it refers to a period. It is very wrong to think that unforgiveness is permissible in any Christian relationship including marital relationships. This is one issue in marriage couples must watch out for. It must be uppermost on your mind that your husband/wife is your brother in Christ. Siblings often refuse to see themselves as brothers in Christ and those who are brothers in Christ refuse to see themselves as family. Such irony!

Forgiveness is a vital aspect in Christianity.

Acts 5:31 Him hath God exalted with his right hand *to be* a Prince and a Saviour, for to give repentance to Israel, and forgiveness of sins.

Acts 13:38 Be it known unto you therefore, men *and* brethren, that through this man is preached unto you the forgiveness of sins:

Colossians 2:13 And you, being dead in your sins and the uncircumcision of your flesh, hath he quickened together with him, having forgiven you all trespasses; Vs13 Forbearing one another, and forgiving one another, if any man have a quarrel against any: even as Christ forgave you, so also do ye.

1 John 2:12 I write unto you, little children, because your sins are forgiven you for his name's sake.

Ephesians 1:7 In whom we have redemption through his blood, the forgiveness of sins, according to the riches of his grace;

Colossians 1:14 In whom we have redemption through his blood, even the forgiveness of sins:

God's action of forgiving the believer ahead of time ought to influence and affect his conduct. No believer can ever justify unforgiveness. It is not of God. It is the most devilish thing that can be retained in the heart.

Interpreting **Matthew 18:18** in the proper context would mean that when a believer finds himself in a situation where he should be offended, he is to bind or restrict the offense, and loose forgiveness.

In other words, even when another doesn't act right, you have a duty to act right. The responsibility to act right is yours. If the other fellow acts like an unbeliever, your corresponding action is to bind unforgiveness. In other words, binding and loosing are the believer's reactions towards offence. It is not just an action, but a reconciliation.

> **Luke 17:1** Then said he unto the disciples, It is impossible but that offences will come: but woe *unto him,* through whom they come!

This means that offences are a constant, they will always come. The word "**offence**" was translated from the Greek word "**aproskopos**" and it means something that causes to stumble. When offences come, rather than focus on the person committing the offence, the believer will do well to see a temptation to stumble. The believer must be prepared in all the relationships that he is involved in, to forgive. Sometimes we put too much pressure on relationships and the bar is raised too high thus giving room for unforgiveness.

Recognize that the people in relationships are flesh and blood! The believer must see forgiveness as his lifestyle and ensure that in all relationships, forgiveness must happen every day. The believer should be ready to practice forgiveness every day. This must be the Believer's worldview as taught in the scriptures.

> **1 John 4:9** In this was manifested the love of God toward us, because that God sent his only begotten Son into the world, that we might live through him. **Vs 10** Herein is love, not that we loved God, but that he loved us, and sent his Son *to be* the propitiation for our sins. **Vs 11** Beloved, if God so loved us, we ought also to

love one another. **Vs 19** We love him, because he first loved us. **Vs 21** And this commandment have we from him, That he who loveth God love his brother also.

When a believer finds himself walking in unforgiveness, it is simply because he has not recognized or has taken his attention off the love of God.

In **Verse 19**, the phrase "**first loved**" was translated from the Greek word "**proton agape**" which implies that the first love is from God to us. When we recognize this, we love others.

Unforgiveness therefore is the lack of appreciation of the gift of God's forgiveness.

Ephesians 4:32 And be ye kind one to another, tenderhearted, forgiving one another, even as God for Christ's sake hath forgiven you.

Paul teaches that what God has done for the believer; he (God) has now made it a nature in him (the believer) so that he can do the same unto others. This places the believer's forgiveness on the platform of God's forgiveness. He has been shown what to do by God's example to him.

Colossians 3:13 Forbearing one another, and forgiving one another, if any man have a **quarrel** against any: even as Christ forgave you, so also *do* ye.

The word "**forbearing**" was translated from the Greek word "**anechomai**" which implies that it will be '**borne**' while the word "**quarrel**" was translated from the Greek word "**momphe,**" which implies to blame, complain or fault

> **Philippians 1:10** That ye may approve things that are excellent; that ye may be sincere and without offence till the day of Christ;

If offence means to cause to stumble or harm, without offence would mean that which will not harm others. Forgiveness is active and not passive, that is why forgiveness without reconciliation is not forgiveness.

Jesus in **Matthew 18** was teaching forgiveness and reconciliation, and not referring to demons in context.

> **Matthew 18:35** So likewise shall my heavenly Father do also unto you, if ye from your hearts forgive not every one his brother their trespasses.

Recall that it is the other party that sinned against you. When you do not forgive, it becomes a sin. If a brother sins against you, when you don't forgive, you sin against God. Unforgiveness is weightier than anything done to you.

Let us look again at the commentaries on forgiveness in the epistles.

Paul.

Romans 12:14 Bless them which persecute you: bless, and curse not. **Vs 15** Rejoice with them that do rejoice, and weep with them that weep. **Vs 16** *Be* of the same mind one toward another. Mind not high things, but condescend to men of low estate. Be not wise in your own conceits. **Vs 17** Recompense to no man evil for evil. Provide things honest in the sight of all men. **Vs 18** If it be possible, as much as lieth in you, live peaceably with all men. **Vs 19** Dearly beloved, avenge not yourselves, but *rather* give place unto wrath: for it is written, Vengeance *is* mine; I will repay, saith the Lord. **Vs 20** Therefore if thine enemy hunger, feed him; if he thirst, give him drink: for in so doing thou shalt heap coals of fire on his head. **Vs 21** Be not overcome of evil, but overcome evil with good.

1 Corinthians 6:2 Do ye not know that the saints shall judge the world? and if the world shall be judged by you, are ye unworthy to judge the smallest matters? **Vs 3** Know ye not that we shall judge angels? how much more things that pertain to this life? **Vs 4** If then ye have judgments of things pertaining to this life, set them to judge who are least esteemed in the church. **Vs 5** I speak to your shame. Is it so, that there is not a wise man among you? no, not one that shall be able to judge between his brethren? **Vs 7** Now therefore there is utterly a fault among you, because ye go to law one with another. Why do ye not rather take wrong? why do ye not rather *suffer yourselves to* be defrauded? **Vs**

8 Nay, ye do wrong, and defraud, and that *your* brethren.

In other words, Paul says it is family business when believers have disagreements. They are to forgive one another. We are not supposed to take our brother(fellow believer) to law court.

2 Corinthians 2:8 Wherefore I beseech you that ye would confirm *your* love toward him. **Vs 9** For to this end also did I write, that I might know the proof of you, whether ye be obedient in all things. **Vs 10** To whom ye forgive any thing, I *forgive* also: for if I forgave any thing, to whom I forgave *it,* for your sakes *forgave I it* in the person of Christ; **Vs 11** Lest Satan should get an advantage of us: for we are not ignorant of his devices.

This was the same brother that he told them to discipline in 1 Corinthians 5

1 Corinthians 5:1 It is reported commonly *that there is* fornication among you, and such fornication as is not so much as named among the Gentiles, that one should have his father's wife. **Vs. 2** And ye are puffed up, and have not rather mourned, that he that hath done this deed might be taken away from among you. **Vs 3** For I verily, as absent in body, but present in spirit, have judged already, as though I were present, *concerning* him that hath so done this deed, **Vs. 4** In the name of our Lord Jesus Christ, when ye are gathered together, and my spirit, with the power of our Lord Jesus

Christ, **Vs. 5** To deliver such an one unto Satan for the destruction of the flesh, that the spirit may be saved in the day of the Lord Jesus. **Vs. 6** Your glorying *is* not good. Know ye not that a little leaven leaveneth the whole lump? **Vs. 7** Purge out therefore the old leaven, that ye may be a new lump, as ye are unleavened. For even Christ our passover is sacrificed for us: **Vs. 8** Therefore let us keep the feast, not with old leaven, neither with the leaven of malice and wickedness; but with the unleavened *bread* of sincerity and truth. **Vs. 9** I wrote unto you in an epistle not to company with fornicators: **Vs. 10** Yet not altogether with the fornicators of this world, or with the covetous, or extortioners, or with idolaters; for then must ye needs go out of the world. **Vs. 11** But now I have written unto you not to keep company, if any man that is called a brother be a fornicator, or covetous, or an idolater, or a railer, or a drunkard, or an extortioner; with such an one no not to eat.

But he still tells them to extend the privileges of fellowship to him.

Galatians 5:13 For, brethren, ye have been called unto liberty; only *use* not liberty for an occasion to the flesh, but by love serve one another. **Vs14** For all the law is fulfilled in one word, *even* in this; Thou shalt love thy neighbour as thyself. **Vs15** But if ye bite and devour one another, take heed that ye be not consumed one of another.

Galatians 6:2 Bear ye one another's burdens, and so fulfil the law of Christ.

Philippians 2:1 If *there be* therefore any consolation in Christ, if any comfort of love, if any fellowship of the Spirit, if any bowels and mercies, **Vs 2** Fulfil ye my joy, that ye be likeminded, having the same love, *being* of one accord, of one mind. **Vs 3** Let nothing *be done* through strife or vainglory; but in lowliness of mind let each esteem other better than themselves.

Ephesians 4:30-32 And grieve not the holy Spirit of God, whereby ye are sealed unto the day of redemption. **Vs** 31 Let all bitterness, and wrath, and anger, and clamour, and evil speaking, be put away from you, with all malice: **Vs** 32 And be ye kind one to another, tenderhearted, forgiving one another, even as God for Christ's sake hath forgiven you

What we say or do to others, the anger and bitterness that is expressed in our reaction to others when we hold on to offences is what grieves the Holy Spirit.

Walking in love, that is, forgiveness, puts away anger and evil speaking. A believer that refuses to walk in love has seared his conscience because the love of God will keep prompting forgiveness and reconciliation.

1 John 3:16 Hereby perceive we the love *of God*, because he laid down his life for us: and we ought to lay down *our* lives for the brethren. **Vs 17** But whoso

> hath this world's good, and seeth his brother have need, and shutteth up his bowels *of compassion* from him, how dwelleth the love of God in him? **Vs 18** My little children, let us not love in word, neither in tongue; but in deed and in truth. **Vs 19** And hereby we know that we are of the truth, and shall assure our hearts before him. **Vs 20** For if our heart condemn us, God is greater than our heart, and knoweth all things. **Vs 21** Beloved, if our heart condemn us not, *then* have we confidence toward God. **Vs 22** And whatsoever we ask, we receive of him, because we keep his commandments, and do those things that are pleasing in his sight. **Vs 23** And this is his commandment, That we should believe on the name of his Son Jesus Christ, and love one another, as he gave us commandment. **Vs 24** And he that keepeth his commandments dwelleth in him, and he in him. And hereby we know that he abideth in us, by the Spirit which he hath given us.

John emphasises the believer's love walk and reminds us that it is based on the love of God for the believer. It is the believer's nature to walk in love. Any action contrary to this, will cause him to be bound in his heart. Unforgiveness is contrary to the nature of the believer.

One of the ways the believer will know he is growing spiritually is how long it takes to forgive another who has wronged him. Recall that the binding and loosing are activities carried out by believers. These are human decisions which not only lead to forgiveness but also reconciliation. The decision is made by the believer. Hence, the love of God does not go to divorce courts. Two believers in a marriage, who walk in love will not push through for a divorce or request a separation. If just one party chooses to walk in love, a lot of times, there will be no fallout.

Unforgiveness is that which breaks a home. Binding and loosing is the believer's reaction. His action is to be active on forgiveness and be inactive on unforgiveness.

Activities in the Local Church

The effect of spiritual growth, in a believer through the process of discipleship, is maturity. This process is carried out in the local church, by the leadership (Pastor). And a basic proof of maturity is being able to transmit the same training to others. This is seen in your words and actions. That is, the understanding you received has changed your mindset and, consequently, a significant shift in your conduct.

Recall what we explained earlier where Paul in (**Ephesians 4:11-15)** shows that spiritual maturity is not a private endeavour, rather a result of training that a believer undergoes in his local church under his Pastor. The text emphasises the very essence of leadership in the local assembly which is to equip the believer to serve one another.

> **Ephesians 4:11** And he gave some, apostles; and some, prophets; and some, evangelists; and some, pastors and teachers; **Vs 12** For the perfecting of the saints, for the work of the ministry, for the edifying of the body of Christ: **Vs 13** Till we all come in the unity of the faith, and of the knowledge of the Son of God, unto a perfect man, unto the measure of the stature of the fulness of Christ: **Vs 14** That we henceforth be no more children, tossed to and fro, and carried about with every wind of doctrine, by the sleight of men, and cunning craftiness, whereby they lie in wait to deceive; **Vs 15** But speaking the truth in love, may grow up into him in all things, which is the head, even Christ:

The local church functions as the training ground for the work of the ministry, that is, where the believer is groomed in the ministry of our Lord Jesus Christ.

This text shows that the expected impact of spiritual growth on a believer is to serve.

It is quite important to know that this is not an afterthought intention of God, God throughout the ages has defined his purpose for man, hence the assembly of God's children is where his activity is well defined.

Notice what He told Moses:

> **Exodus 4:22** And thou shalt say unto Pharaoh, Thus saith the Lord, Israel is my son, even my firstborn: **Vs 23** And I say unto thee, Let my son go, that he may

> serve me: and if thou refuse to let him go, behold, I will slay thy son, even thy firstborn.

Israel was called out of Egypt to serve God. Looking at the book Exodus, the purpose of God's deliverance of Israel through Moses is to serve him. This fact was first seen in God's commandment to Adam to tend and keep the Garden (as explained earlier in this book). We see God's appearance to different generations seeking to reveal and execute his purpose through man.

God was undeterred by the short comings of men throughout the ages. He will seek out and find men in every generation to partner and work with to bring his plan to pass in the earth.

He chose Israel as a nation and chose Moses as their leader.

> **Exodus 3:11** And Moses said unto God, Who am I, that I should go unto Pharaoh, and that I should bring forth the children of Israel out of Egypt? **Vs 12** And he said, Certainly I will be with thee; and this shall be a token unto thee, that I have sent thee: When thou hast brought forth the people out of Egypt, **ye shall serve God upon this mountain.**

Thus, God delivered Israel from bondage in Egypt to serve Him. In other words, God's plan and purpose for man is to serve Him.

Therefore, Sonship in God's kingdom is for service. Notice what God said further:

> **Exodus 19:6** And ye shall be unto me a kingdom of priests, and an holy nation. These are the words which thou shalt speak unto the children of Israel.

He wanted them to be a kingdom of priests in the whole earth. This was the same plan God had from the book of Genesis. Every one of them is expected to be God's servant.

The primary reason or essence of the local Church is spiritual growth, and the proof of this is that that believer will be actively and effectively involved in the work of the ministry.

What are the activities in the local church?

1. Preaching

This is one of the prominent activity in the local assembly.

> **Act 6:4** But we will give ourselves continually to prayer, and to the ministry of the word.

Apostles here said they will give themselves continually to the ministry of the word.

Ministry of the word here refers to preaching and teaching.

> **Act 6:8** And Stephen, full of faith and power, did great wonders and miracles among the people. **Vs,** 9 Then there arose certain of the synagogue, which is called *the synagogue* of the Libertines, and Cyrenians, and Alexandrians, and of them of Cilicia and of Asia, disputing with Stephen. **Vs,** 10 And they were not able to resist the wisdom and the spirit by which he spake.

Stephen one of the deacon was found preaching.

During martyr of Stephen and persecution of the church, the believers were found preaching every where they went to. It is so important that even persecution did not make them to keep shut, rather a means to spread the gospel.

> **Act 11:19** Now they which were scattered abroad upon the persecution that arose about Stephen travelled as far as Phenice, and Cyprus, and Antioch, preaching the word to none but unto the Jews only

> **Act 13:4** So they, being sent forth by the Holy Ghost, departed unto Seleucia; and from thence they sailed to Cyprus. **Vs. 5** And when they were at Salamis, they preached the word of God in the synagogues of the Jews: and they had also John to *their* minister.

> **Act 16:10** And after he had seen the vision, immediately we endeavoured to go into Macedonia, assuredly gathering that the Lord had called us for to preach the gospel unto them.

Act 11:20 And some of them were men of Cyprus and Cyrene, which, when they were come to Antioch, spake unto the Grecians, preaching the Lord Jesus.

Act 15:35 Paul also and Barnabas continued in Antioch, teaching and preaching the word of the Lord, with many others also.

Act 20:25 And now, behold, I know that ye all, among whom I have gone preaching the kingdom of God, shall see my face no more.

Act 28:31 Preaching the kingdom of God, and teaching those things which concern the Lord Jesus Christ, with all confidence, no man forbidding him.

Preaching is an important activity in the local assembly. We saw the Paul even in the chains kept preaching the gospel. Preaching must be going on the local church on a regular basis.

Paul charged a pastor:

2 Timothy 4:1 I charge *thee* therefore before God, and the Lord Jesus Christ, who shall judge the quick and the dead at his appearing and his kingdom; **Vs. 2** Preach the word; be instant in season, out of season; reprove, rebuke, exhort with all longsuffering and doctrine.

The believer has been given a mandate to preach, by the Lord Jesus.

2 Corinthians 5:17 Therefore if any man be in Christ, he is a new creature: old things are passed away; behold, all things are become new. Vs 18 And all things are of God, who hath reconciled us to himself by Jesus Christ, and hath given to us the ministry of reconciliation Vs 19 To wit, that God was in Christ, reconciling the world unto himself, not imputing their trespasses unto them; and hath committed unto us the word of reconciliation. Vs 20 Now then we are ambassadors for Christ, as though God did beseech you by us: we pray you in Christ's stead, be Ye reconciled to God.

The ministry of reconciliation has been giving to every believer. This was exactly what Jesus told his disciples.

Matthew 28:18 And Jesus came and spake unto them, saying, All power is given unto me in heaven and in earth. Va 19 Go ye therefore, and teach all nations, baptizing them in the name of the Father, and of the Son, and of the Holy Ghost: Vs 20 Teaching them to observe all things whatsoever I have commanded you: and, lo, I am with you alway, even unto the end of the world. Amen.

Mark 16:14 Afterward he appeared unto the eleven a9 they sat at meat, and upbraided them with their unbelief and hardness of heart, because they believed not them which had seen him after he was risen. V3 15 And he said unto them, Go ye into all the world, and preach the gospel to every creature. '

Every believer has been given a teaching and preaching ministry.

> Romans 12:11 Not slothful in business; fervent in spirit; serving the Lord;

> 1st Corinthians 15:58 Therefore, my beloved brethren, be ye stedfast, unmoveable, always abounding in the work of the Lord, forasmuch as ye know that your labour is not in vain in the Lord.

A believer who is growing spiritually will be involved in evangelism preaching and teaching, the essence of the training is for him to be involved in preaching and teaching.

2. Prayer

This is another important activity in the local church. The believer must be actively involved in prayer as he grows and embarks on the work of the ministry.

The Apostles strongly affirmed this:

> **Acts 6: 2** Then the twelve called the multitude of the disciples unto them, and said, It is not reason that we should leave the word of God, and serve tables.. 4 But we will give ourselves continually to prayer, and to the ministry of the word.

Jesus gave them those instructions to pray always.

Luke 18:1 And he spake a parable unto them *to this end,* that men ought always to pray, and not to faint;

The Apostles and the disciples in the book of Acts were given to prayer.

Act 1:13 And when they were come in, they went up into an upper room, where abode both Peter, and James, and John, and Andrew, Philip, and Thomas, Bartholomew, and Matthew, James *the son* of Alphaeus, and Simon Zelotes, and Judas *the brother* of James. **V. 14** These all continued with one accord in prayer and supplication, with the women, and Mary the mother of Jesus, and with his brethren.

Act 2:42 And they continued stedfastly in the apostles' doctrine and fellowship, and in breaking of bread, and in prayers.

Act 3:1 Now Peter and John went up together into the temple at the hour of prayer, *being* the ninth *hour.*

Act 4:24 And when they heard that, they lifted up their voice to God with one accord, and said, Lord, thou *art* God, which hast made heaven, and earth, and the sea, and all that in them is:

Act 10:9 On the morrow, as they went on their journey, and drew nigh unto the city, Peter went up upon the housetop to pray about the sixth hour:

Act 12:5 Peter therefore was kept in prison: but prayer was made without ceasing of the church unto God for him.

Clearly the church in the book of Acts was given to prayer.

Paul:

1Timothy 2:1 I exhort therefore, that, first of all, supplications, prayers, intercessions, *and* giving of thanks, be made for all men;

"First of all" shows that it is a primary activity.

What were they praying for?

- They prayed for boldness to preach (Act 4:24).

Paul also taught the same.

Ephesians 6:19 And for me, that utterance may be given unto me, that I may open my mouth boldly, to make known the mystery of the gospel, **Vs, 20** For which I am an ambassador in bonds: that therein I may speak boldly, as I ought to speak.

Colossians 4:3 Withal praying also for us, that God would open unto us a door of utterance, to speak the mystery of Christ, for which I am also in bonds: **Vs. 4** That I may make it manifest, as I ought to speak.

- They prayed for the deliverance of Peter (a minister of the gospel) (Act 12:5)

Paul also taught the same.

Romans 15:30 Now I beseech you, brethren, for the Lord Jesus Christ's sake, and for the love of the Spirit, that ye strive together with me in *your* prayers to God for me;

Romans 15:30 Now I beseech you, brethren, for the Lord Jesus Christ's sake, and for the love of the Spirit, that ye strive together with me in *your* prayers to God for me; **Vs.** 31 That I may be delivered from them that do not believe in Judaea; and that my service which *I have* for Jerusalem may be accepted of the saints; **Vs. 31** That I may be delivered from them that do not believe in Judaea; and that my service which *I have* for Jerusalem may be accepted of the saints;

Phillipians 1:19 For I know that this shall turn to my salvation through your prayer, and the supply of the Spirit of Jesus Christ,

2nd Thessalonians 3:1 Finally, brethren, pray for us, that the word of the Lord may have *free* course, and be glorified, even as *it is* with you: **Vs. 2** Finally, brethren, pray for us, that the word of the Lord may have *free*

course, and be glorified, even as *it is* with you: **Vs.** 3 And that we may be delivered from unreasonable and wicked men: for all *men* have not faith.

- For fellow believers.

Ephesians 6:18 Praying always with all prayer and supplication in the Spirit, and watching thereunto with all perseverance and supplication for all saints

Ephesians 1:16 Cease not to give thanks for you, making mention of you in my prayers; **Vs. 17** That the God of our Lord Jesus Christ, the Father of glory, may give unto you the spirit of wisdom and revelation in the knowledge of him: **Vs.** 18 The eyes of your understanding being enlightened; that ye may know what is the hope of his calling, and what the riches of the glory of his inheritance in the saints,

Philippians 1:9 And this I pray, that your love may abound yet more and more in knowledge and *in* all judgment; **Vs.10** That ye may approve things that are excellent; that ye may be sincere and without offence till the day of Christ; **Vs.**11 Being filled with the fruits of righteousness, which are by Jesus Christ, unto the glory and praise of God.

Colossians 1:9 For this cause we also, since the day we heard *it,* do not cease to pray for you, and to desire that ye might be filled with the knowledge of his will in all wisdom and spiritual understanding; **Vs. 10** That ye might walk worthy of the Lord unto all pleasing, being fruitful in every good work, and increasing in the knowledge of God;

Philemon 1:4 I thank my God, making mention of thee always in my prayers, **Vs. 5** Hearing of thy love and faith, which thou hast toward the Lord Jesus, and toward all saints; **Vs.** 6 That the communication of thy faith may become effectual by the acknowledging of every good thing which is in you in Christ Jesus.

Epaphras laboured always in prayer for believers in Colossae.

Colossians 4:12 Epaphras, who is one of you, a servant of Christ, saluteth you, always labouring fervently for you in prayers, that ye may stand perfect and complete in all the will of God. V8 13 For I bear him record, that he hath a great zeal for you, and them that are in Laodicea, and them in Hierapolis

Notice the use of the word always to show how often believer prays.

1st Thessalonians 5:17 Pray without ceasing.

Prayer is a constant activity of the believer in the local church. Prayer makes the believer function effectively in God's will and purpose. Every believer should be involved in the prayer meeting of the local church he or she belongs to.

Giving

Giving is one of the activities in the local church, taught by the apostles. And we saw it as the practice of the local assembly in the book of Acts..

> **Act 2:44** And all that believed were together, and had all things common; **Vs.** 45 And sold their possessions and goods, and parted them to all *men,* as every man had need. **Vs.** 46 And they, continuing daily with one accord in the temple, and breaking bread from house to house, did eat their meat with gladness and singleness of heart,

They gave to meet the need of others.

> **Act 4:34** Neither was there any among them that lacked: for as many as were possessors of lands or houses sold them, and brought the prices of the things that were sold, **Vs 35** And laid *them* down at the apostles' feet: and distribution was made unto every man according as he had need. **Vs 36** And Joses, who by the apostles was surnamed Barnabas, (which is, being interpreted, The son of consolation,) a Levite, *and* of the country of Cyprus, **Vs. 37** Having land, sold *it,* and brought the money, and laid *it* at the apostles' feet.

Paul gave specific instructions to local Churches to give.

> **Act 20:33** I have coveted no man's silver, or gold, or apparel. **Vs** 34 Yea, ye yourselves know, that these

hands have ministered unto my necessities, and to them that were with me. **Vs** 35 I have shewed you all things, how that so labouring ye ought to support the weak, and to remember the words of the Lord Jesus, how he said, It is more blessed to give than to receive.

1st Corinthians 16:1 Now concerning the collection for the saints, as I have given order to the Churches of Galatia, even so do ye. Vs 2 Upon the first day of the week let every one of you lay by him in store, as God hath prospered him, that there be no gatherings when I come.

He instructed them to give weekly; the first day of the week!

..."Upon the first day of the week let every one of you lay by him in store, as he hath prospered him, that there be no gatherings when I come.

The Believer's giving in to the local Church ought to be commensurate with his income. That is, the more I have, the more I give.

Paul in Chapter 8 and 9 spoke highly about the church that was involve in Giving.

2nd Corinthians 9:6 But this I say, He which soweth sparingly shall reap also sparingly; and he which soweth bountifully shall reap also bountifully. V8 7 Every man according as he purposeth in his heart, so let him give; not grudgingly, or of necessity: for God loveth a cheerful giver.

2nd Corinthians 8:1 Moreover, brethren, we do you to wit of the grace of God bestowed on the Churches of Macedonia; Vs 2 How that in a great trial of affliction the abundance of their joy and their deep poverty abounded unto the riches of their liberality. Vs 3 For to their power, I bear record, yea, and beyond their power they were willing of themselves; Vs 4 Praying us with much intreaty that we would receive the gift, and take upon us the fellowship of the ministering to the saints. Vs 5 And this they did, not as We hoped, but first gave their own selves to the Lord, and unto us by the will of God. Vs 6 Insomuch that we desired Titus, that as he had begun, so he would also finish in you the same grace also.

He notes that giving in the local church should be done cheerfully and not grudgingly, you are to determine what to give before you come for the service and It should be done sacrificially

Therefore, giving in Christian meetings therefore ought to be systematic and not incidental. Giving. to our Local Church (Our Pastors and leaders, fellow believers,) is an integral part of the activities in the local church.

Who/What do we give to?

- Ministers of the Gospel.

1st Corinthians 9:11 If we have sown unto you spirituall things, is it a great thing if we shall reap your carnal things? Vs 12 If others be partakers of this power over you, are not we rather? Nevertheless we have not used this power; but suffer all things, lest we should hinder the gospel of Christ. Vs 13 Do ye not know that they which .minister about holy things live of the things of the temple? and they Which wait at the altar are partakers with the altar? Vs 14 Even so hath the Lord ordained that they which preach the gospel should live of the gospel.

Galatians 6:6 Let him that is taught in the word communicate unto him that teacheth in all good things.

1st Timothy 5:17 Let the elders that rule well be counted worthy of double honour, especially they who labour in the word and doctrine. Vs 18 For the scripture saith, Thou shalt not muzzle the ox that treadeth out the corn. And, The labourer is worthy of his reward.

He explained that the response of believers to having been ministered to or blessed by a minister of the gospel, is to bless that minister materially. It is the responsibility of the church to take care of their Pastor. This is how we honour that minister.

2nd Corinthians 8:2 How that in a great trial of affliction the abundance of their joy and their deep poverty abounded unto the riches of their liberality. Vs

3 For to their power, I bear record, yea, and beyond their power they were willing of themselves; V3 4 Praying us with much intreaty that we would receive the gift, and take upon us the fellowship of the ministering to the saints. V8 5 And this they did, not as we hoped, 'but first gave their own selves to the Lord, and unto us by the will of God.

Philippians 4:10 But I rejoiced in the Lord greatly, that now at the last your care of me hath flourished again; wherein ye were also careful, but ye lacked Opportunity. Vs 11 Not that I speak in respect of want: for I have learned, in whatsoever state I am, therewith to be content. Vs 121 know both how to be abased, and I know how to abound: everywhere and in all things I am instructed both to be full and to be hungry, both to abound and to suffer need. Vs 13 I can do all things through Christ which strengtheneth me. V3 14 Notwithstanding ye have well done, that ye did communicate with my affliction. Vs 15 Now ye Philippians know also, that in the beginning of the gospel, when I departed from Macedonia, no Church communicated with me as concerning giving and receiving, but ye only. Vs 16 For even in Thessalonica ye sent once and again unto my necessity. Vs 17 Not because I desire a gift: but I desire fruit that may abound to your account. Vs 18 But I have all, and abound: I am full having received of Epaphroditus the things which were sent from you, an odour of a sweet smell, a sacrifice acceptable, wellpleasing to God.

You will notice how Paul spoke highly of the churches the ministered to them. Observe that because they were demanding for it but they acted according to the commandment of God in the scripture and Paul commended them for that. So the believers ought to give to their Pastors and leader, as the scripture instructed.

- To fellow believers.

Act 2:44 And all that believed were together, and had all things common; **Vs. 45** And sold their possessions and goods, and parted them to all *men,* as every man had need.

Act 4:34 Neither was there any among them that lacked: for as many as were possessors of lands or houses sold them, and brought the prices of the things that were sold, **Vs. 35** And laid *them* down at the apostles' feet: and distribution was made unto every man according as he had need. **Vs.** 36 And Joses, who by the apostles was surnamed Barnabas, (which is, being interpreted, The son of consolation,) a Levite, *and* of the country of Cyprus, **Vs.** 37 Having land, sold *it,* and brought the money, and laid *it* at the apostles' feet.

Galatians 6:10 As we have therefore opportunity, let us do good unto all men, especially unto them who are of the household of faith.

Ephesians 4:28 Let him that stole steal no more: but rather let him labour, working with his hands the thing which is good, that he may have to give to him that needeth.

1st Thessalonians 5:14 Now we exhort you, brethren, warn them that are unruly, comfort the feebleminded, support the weak, be patient toward all men.

The believer must be devoted; dedicated; committed; steadfast towards supporting one another. There is no selfishness in the local assembly. The local church destroys selfishness and individualism in the believer. We ought to serve one another in love. This was exactly what the early church practiced in the book of Acts 3 and 4.

- To meet the needs of the Church

Paul spoke about Gaius' benevolence

Romans 16:23 Gaius mine host, and of the whole Church, saluteth you. Erastus the Chamberlain of the city saluteth you, and Quartus a brother.

John said the same concerning Gaius.

3rd John 1:5 Beloved, thou doest faithfully whatsoever thou doest to the brethren, and to strangers; Vs 6 Which have home witness of thy charity before the Church: whom if thou bring forward on their journey after a godly sort, thou shalt do well:

So, Gaius was known to support the local Church materially. Thus, the need of the local Church is the responsibility of the believers. We have a duty to give to meet the needs of our local Church.

1st Peter 4:8 And above all things have fervent charity among yourselves: for charity shall cover the multitude of sins. Vs 9 Use hospitality one to another without grudging.

1st John 3:16 Hereby perceive we the love of God, because he laid down his life for us: and we ought to lay down our lives for the brethren. Vs 17 But whoso hath this world's good, and seeth his brother have need, and shutteth up his bowels of compassion from him, how dwelleth the love of God in him? Vs 18 My little children, let us not love in word, neither in tongue; but in deed and in truth. Vs 19 And hereby we know that we are of the truth, and shall assure our hearts before him.

Acts 4:32 And the multitude of them that believed were of one heart and of one soul: neither said any of them that ought of the things which he possessed was his own; but they had all things common. V8 33 And with great power gave the apostles witness of the resurrection of the Lord Jesus: and great grace was upon them all. Vs 34 Neither was there any among them that lacked: for as many as were possessors of lands or houses sold them, and brought the prices of the things that were sold, Vs 35 And laid then/ down at the apostles' feet: and distribution was made unto every man according as he had need. Vs 36 And loses, who by the apostles was surnamed Barnabas, (which is, being interpreted, The son of consolation,) a Levite, and of the country of Cyprus, Vs 37 Having land, sold it, and brought the money, and laid it at the apostles' feet.

This is very similar to Acts 2 above. Luke in Verse 34 state the fact they brought what they are giving to the Apostles for the distribution to the needs of the Saints.

Acts 11:28 And there stood up one of them named Agabus, and signified by the Spirit that there should be great dearth throughout all the world: which came to pass in the days of Claudius Caesar. Vs 29 Then the disciples, every man according to his ability, determined to send relief unto the brethren which dwelt in Iudaea: Vs 30 Which also they did; and sent it to the elders by the hands of Barnabas and Saul.

The word "ability" implies believers gave according to how prosperous they were." In all, it was their choice to determine how much they gave. The word "determined" implies they all gave willingly.

Acts 20:35 I have shewed you all things, how that so labouring ye ought to support the weak, and to remember the words of the Lord Jesus, how he said, It is more blessed to give than to receive. **VS. 34** Yea, ye

> yourselves know, that these hands; have ministered unto my necessities, and to them that Were with me.

Thus, the weak in context would refer to believers in need. Believers ought to generously give to meet the needs of one another.

It is clear that this attitude was consistent in the book of Acts. Believers sold their possessions and gave generously for the distribution to the saints. Giving is very important in the local church. The needs of the church are meat by the members of the local church. And giving is also a proof of maturity.

Matured believers are ordained into Ministry (ministry of laying on of hands)

> **Act 6:2** Then the twelve called the multitude of the disciples *unto them,* and said, It is not reason that we should leave the word of God, and serve tables. **Vs.** 3 Wherefore, brethren, look ye out among you seven men of honest report, full of the Holy Ghost and wisdom, whom we may appoint over this business. **Vs.** 4 But we will give ourselves continually to prayer, and to the ministry of the word. **Vs.**:5 And the saying pleased the whole multitude: and they chose Stephen, a man full of faith and of the Holy Ghost, and Philip, and Prochorus, and Nicanor, and Timon, and Parmenas, and Nicolas a proselyte of Antioch: **Vs.** 6 Whom they set before the apostles: and when they had prayed, they laid *their*

hands on them. **Vs.** 7 And the word of God increased; and the number of the disciples multiplied in Jerusalem greatly; and a great company of the priests were obedient to the faith. **Vs.** 8 And Stephen, full of faith and power, did great wonders and miracles among the people. **Vs.** 9 Then there arose certain of the synagogue, which is called *the synagogue* of the Libertines, and Cyrenians, and Alexandrians, and of them of Cilicia and of Asia, disputing with Stephen. **Vs.** 10 And they were not able to resist the wisdom and the spirit by which he spake.

Notice that the ordination of the 7 deacons here also increased the impact of the church at Jerusalem as seen in Vs 7. We also see that Stephen preached boldly.

Observe also that this happened after the Apostles **laid hands** on them

One of the deacon Philip that was ordained at **Acts 6**. also went to preach at Samaria.

Act 8:5 Then Philip went down to the city of Samaria, and preached Christ unto them. **Vs:6** And the people with one accord gave heed unto those things which Philip spake, hearing and seeing the miracles which he did.

Act 13:1 Now there were in the church that was at Antioch certain prophets and teachers; as Barnabas, and Simeon that was called Niger, and Lucius of Cyrene, and Manaen, which had been brought up with Herod the tetrarch, and Saul. **Vs.** 2 As they ministered to the Lord, and fasted, the Holy Ghost said, Separate me Barnabas and Saul for the work whereunto I have called them. **Vs.**:3 And when they had fasted and prayed, and laid *their* hands on them, they sent *them* away. **Vs.** 4 So they, being sent forth by the Holy Ghost, departed unto Seleucia; and from thence they sailed to Cyprus.

The leaders in the local church at Antioch laid hands on Paul and Barnabas and send them fourth to do the work of the ministry. Notice that prior to this time they have been preaching but not in the way they did after they sent forth by laying on of hand. That defines the direction of their ministry to them.

Paul twice reminded Timothy of the hands that was laid on him by the leadership of the church.

1Timothy 4:14 Neglect not the gift that is in thee, which was given thee by prophecy, with the laying on of the hands of the presbytery.

2 Timothy 1:6 Wherefore I put thee in remembrance that thou stir up the gift of God, which is in thee by the putting on of my hands.

Timothy was a minister of the Gospel and Paul here told him to always remember that event of laying on of hand by the leadership of the church.

> **1 Timothy:21** I charge *thee* before God, and the Lord Jesus Christ, and the elect angels, that thou observe these things without preferring one before another, doing nothing by partiality. **Vs. 22** Lay hands suddenly on no man, neither be partaker of other men's sins: keep thyself pure.

Here Paul instructs timothy not to put people into leadership position in a hurry. So laying on of hands play an important role in ordaining the believer to function in the work of the ministry

> **Titus 1:4** To Titus, *mine* own son after the common faith: Grace, mercy, *and* peace, from God the Father and the Lord Jesus Christ our Saviour. Vs 5 For this cause left I thee in Crete, that thou shouldest set in order the things that are wanting, and ordain elders in every city, as I had appointed thee:

Hence we can infer that Titus is expected to ordain elders in every city just like the Apostles did, by laying hands on them, this brings direction and effectiveness in the call of god upon the lives of the Believer. Hence the believer seek and endeavour that hands are laid on him as he embarks in the work of the ministry.

Conclusively. The local church represents God's wisdom and plays a pivotal role in the life of the believer. It serves as the pillar and ground of truth, where individuals come into contact with the revelation of God and His plan for the earth. Through consistent attendance at this physical gathering, believers receive this ministry as a result of discipleship, which includes teaching and instruction. This is evidenced in their service to others, as observed in the aforementioned activities.

CHAPTER 4

THE LOCAL CHURCH AND THIS WORLD

Recall that in the previous chapters, we have endeavoured to present the truth of God's word, that is, bible definitions and explanations about what the church is, what the local church is and what it is not. We have also examined the role of the local church and its activities.

Furthermore, a major truth about the church and the local church that we cannot over-emphasize is how the local church is that PHYSICAL expression of the body of Christ in the earth today, that is, the very core of what is called the local church is that it is an assembly or a gathering of believers with definite leadership and structure that fosters spiritual growth, submission, accountability and training via discipleship. Hence, in the previous chapters, we clearly explained that there is no such thing as an "online church" or a "new normal" of 'doing church'. Such phrases are an aberration and a revisionism of clear scriptural instructions to gather as believers.

To hold a different view from what the scriptures clearly teach about this, as a believer or as a local church, is to hold or promote a secular or a non-biblical worldview where we think that the local church can be subjected to the whims and caprices of what is acceptable, popular or convenient in today's world.

In this chapter, we intend to present or re-present what the local church is, our worldview as members of the local church and how we are to relate with or interact with the world that we live in without being wrongly influenced or losing our identity to this world.

To begin with, the church has its own cultures and traditions that we must uphold throughout the ages.

> **1 Corinthians 11:1-2** Be ye followers of me, even as I also *am* of Christ. Vs 2 Now I praise you, brethren, that ye remember me in all things, and keep the ordinances, as I delivered *them* to you.

In the text quoted above, it is clear that Paul delivered unto them clear instructions, ordinances or traditions that they were to uphold even as they interact with their world or the culture of their day in Corinth then.

This implies that whilst we can seek to understand a culture or a generation (particularly so as to reach them better with the gospel), we are not expected to adopt those cultures or adapt to this generation. We have been sent by God into the world, not to conform to the world but to transform it. We are to transform the different generations of men with God's word, showing them God's purposes and plans for and in the earth, not conform or adapt God's word to whatever generation we find ourselves in.

Furthermore, the institution of the local church is a pivotal aspect of God's wisdom in orchestrating healthy and functional human interactions. Within this assembly called the local church is the opportunity for believers to come together to worship, support one another and grow spiritually. The local church encapsulates God's design for collective worship, mutual edification and the communal expression of faith.

Again, observe the emphasis on community which is a core value or objective of the local church, hence the emphasis on physical gatherings and/or assemblies. Our union in/with Christ (called the body of Christ) already ties us together with other believers in Christ. Thus, like we have said earlier, a fundamental fact we have seen in this study is the constant emphasis on the physical gathering of believers in an assembly called the local church. What is called the online church is an anomaly, an exigency or an expediency of a dire time (such as the recent COVID-19 pandemic or cases of extreme persecution) that shouldn't be made the norm.

As believers and as a local church, it is imperative for us to note very distinctly that though we are in the world, we are not of this world

John 18:36 Jesus answered, My kingdom is not of this world: if my kingdom were of this world, then would my servants fight, that I should not be delivered to the Jews: but now is my kingdom not from hence.

Jesus was very clear about his kingdom being different from the world's kingdom and the believer in Christ, by virtue of redemption has been translated into the kingdom of Christ.

Colossians 1:13 Who hath delivered us from the power of darkness, and hath translated *us* into the kingdom of his dear Son:

The church of Christ is that universal body or union where Jesus is the head and we (the believers) are his body. The church therefore is where that kingdom of Christ, his reign and authority are mirrored, displayed, demonstrated and exercised.

The local church is what we can refer to as the physical expression of the kingdom of Christ in all of the earth. This means that in the world today, the church (or the local church) can be described as God's answer to a distorted, dysfunctional or disorderly world. It means that via the church (or the local church) God seeks to restore order and functionality to his creation such that issues like racism, gender bias, classism and other anomalies in human interactions and relations is corrected via the truth of God's word as taught and practiced by believers in the different local assemblies around the world.

For instance, in Matthew 20

> **Matthew 20:25-28** But Jesus called them *unto him,* and said, Ye know that the princes of the Gentiles exercise dominion over them, and they that are great exercise authority upon them. Vs 26 But it shall not be so among you: but whosoever will be great among you, let him be your minister; Vs 27 And whosoever will be chief among you, let him be your servant: Vs 28 Even as the Son of man came not to be ministered unto, but to minister, and to give his life a ransom for many.

Jesus clearly shows us that there is a difference between the way the world sees greatness and exercises authority and the way the Church (his body) should see greatness and exercise authority. In the church, we are taught that greatness is service, that is, when we serve, we are already great in the kingdom of God.

In the body of Christ, we do not have races, gender discrimination or inequality, societal, ethnical or political classes or differences.

> **Galatians 3:26-28** For ye are all the children of God by faith in Christ Jesus. [27] For as many of you as have been baptized into Christ have put on Christ. [28] There is neither Jew nor Greek, there is neither bond nor free, there is neither male nor female: for ye are all one in Christ Jesus.

Rather, what we have are men and women, young and old, small or great, rich or poor, from different walks of life and classes who are bound together by faith in Christ and service to the Lord. In this union, our classes or differences in the natural do not impede our supernatural relationships such that we do not address each other by whatever we are in the natural, rather, what we have amongst us (in the local church) is leadership (via service or ministry) and the essence is to show example to also train other believers to do what the leaders are doing based on maturity.

However, we cannot but also address a growing trend and concern amongst believers and even leaders in the local churches today. In relating with or interacting with the world that we live in, whether consciously or unconsciously, we have started grooming a set of believers who do not have a strictly biblical worldview but have either a totally secular worldview or a syncretic or syncretistic worldview. This fact is further expressed by research carried out by George Barna as captured below

> "As veteran researcher and CRC Director of Research George Barna explains, "It's just further evidence that the culture is influencing the American church much more than Christian churches are influencing the culture."

According to this report, the level of biblical worldview varies by the pastoral position held. Among Senior Pastors, for instance, 41% hold a biblical worldview—the highest incidence among any of the five pastoral positions studied. Next highest was the 28% among Associate Pastors. One of the more concerning revelations emerging from the research is the worldview of pastors who work with young people, Barna noted. The study found that only 12% of Children's and Youth Pastors hold a biblical worldview. And among Teaching Pastors, the level of biblical worldview is a mere 13%.

> "A person's worldview primarily develops before the age of 13, then goes through a period of refinement during their teens and twenties. Therefore, from a worldview development perspective, a church's most important ministers are the Children's Pastor and the Youth Pastor," Barna said.

> "Discovering that seven out of every eight of those pastors lack a biblical worldview helps to explain why so few among the nation's youngest generations are developing a heart and mind for biblical principles and ways of life, and why our society seems to have run wild over the last decade," Barna explained.

According to ACU President Len Munsil, the findings highlight that the biblical worldview crisis in America begins at the top.

> "Our latest research shows this is stunning erosion of biblical understanding is present even among the leaders of the Church," Munsil said. "We need a

comprehensive strategy to rebuild biblical worldview into every generation and in every part of life," Munsil said. "For ACU, this means strategically training our students to develop a biblical worldview through their academic curriculum, spiritual formation programs, and co-curricular activities. And through CRC, we continue to identify ways to build biblical worldview throughout the church, in families and throughout our culture."

The latest report from the AWVI 2022 found that the prevailing worldview among pastors is best described as Syncretism, the blending of ideas and applications from a variety of holistic worldviews into a unique but inconsistent combination that represents their personal preferences.

More than six of every 10 pastors (62%) hold a syncretistic worldview. This trend is also being seen more widely in American culture, with almost nine out of 10 U.S. adults (88%) embracing Syncretism as their primary worldview[9].

We cannot afford to hold and promote the same worldviews with unbelievers or non-believers otherwise we will lose a firm grip on our identity and purpose as

---

[9] Barna, G.; Muncil, T. F. 2022 New Study Shows Shocking Lack of Biblical Worldview Among American Pastors [online]. Available at: https://www.arizonachristian.edu/2022/05/12/shocking-lack-of-biblical-worldview-among-american-pastors/ [Accessed: March 21, 2024]

defined within the scriptures. Paul writes strongly to distinct the believer from the unbeliever as quoted below.

> **2 Corinthians 6:14-17** Be ye not unequally yoked together with unbelievers: for what fellowship hath righteousness with unrighteousness? and what communion hath light with darkness? [15] And what concord hath Christ with Belial? or what part hath he that believeth with an infidel? [16] And what agreement hath the temple of God with idols? for ye are the temple of the living God; as God hath said, I will dwell in them, and walk in them ; and I will be their God, and they shall be my people. [17] Wherefore come out from among them, and be ye separate, saith the Lord, and touch not the unclean thing ; and I will receive you,

We are strongly taught and admonished here to be separate from or not to be unequally yoked together with unbelievers. This means that believers and by extension the local church must know how to interact with the world that we are in, that is, we must know how to engage; to have contact without contamination or corruption.

This is why, now, more than ever before, the believer and the local churches as whole must take very seriously, Paul's admonition in the book of Romans, the 12th chapter.

> **Romans 12:1-2** I beseech you therefore, brethren, by the mercies of God, that ye present your bodies a living sacrifice, holy, acceptable unto God, which is your reasonable service. [2] And be not conformed to this

world: but be ye transformed by the renewing of your mind, that ye may prove what is that good, and acceptable, and perfect, will of God.

The overall admonition here is for a continual renewing or re-education of the mind (of believers) such that we are able to prove what is the perfect and acceptable will of God

What then is the Will of God for the Local Church?

God's will today is the same one he has had all through the ages which is for man to proclaim his message, his kingdom, his gospel in all the earth, that is, his will for the local church can be summed up in what is today referred to as the great commission

Matthew 28:18-20 And Jesus came and spake unto them, saying, All power is given unto me in heaven and in earth. [19] Go ye therefore, and teach all nations, baptizing them in the name of the Father, and of the Son, and of the Holy Ghost: [20] Teaching them to observe all things whatsoever I have commanded you: and, lo, I am with you alway, even unto the end of the world. Amen.

Mark 16:15-18 And he said unto them, Go ye into all the world, and preach the gospel to every creature. [16] He that believeth and is baptized shall be saved; but he that believeth not shall be damned. [17] And these signs shall follow them that believe; In my name shall they cast out devils; they shall speak with new tongues; [18] They shall take up serpents; and if they drink any deadly thing, it shall not hurt them; they shall lay hands on the sick, and they shall recover.

Luke 24:47-48 And that repentance and remission of sins should be preached in his name among all nations, beginning at Jerusalem. [48] And ye are witnesses of these things.

John 20:21-23 Then said Jesus to them again, Peace be unto you: as my Father hath sent me, even so send I you. [22] And when he had said this, he breathed on them, and saith unto them, Receive ye the Holy Ghost: [23] Whose soever sins ye remit, they are remitted unto them; and whose soever sins ye retain, they are retained.

Acts 1:8 But ye shall receive power, after that the Holy Ghost is come upon you: and ye shall be witnesses unto me both in Jerusalem, and in all Judaea, and in Samaria, and unto the uttermost part of the earth.

This means that the role of the local church in this world is to make disciples of all the nations or of every creature, that is, to get men saved, filled with the Holy ghost and ultimately to disciple them such that they are able to replicate this, that is, they are able to get others saved who will get others saved till the whole earth is reached and discipled with the gospel of Christ

Therefore, the church or the local church ought to be primarily focused on this and cautiously relate with the world to ward off any unholy influence or practices. This is why it is abnormal to try to use gimmicks, entertainment or comedy to groom believers in the church rather than train them and nurture them to grow and serve and do the work of ministry. Every local church ought to be a bible school where believers are raised to be able to reach the world with the gospel of Christ; a place where everyone can speak like the apostles of old that we will rather give ourselves to prayer and the ministry of the word than comedy or entertainment.

- The Local Church and earthly Authorities

Earthly authorities or human governments have since been found in scriptures, that is, right from Genesis and a key thing to note is that they are man-made. Human governments and innovations can be found in Genesis

> **Genesis 4:16** And Cain went out from the presence of the CORD, and dwelt in the land of Nod, on the east of Eden

Cain sought to do that which was pleasing in his eyes. Nimrod was also likewise mentioned.

> **Genesis 10:8-9** And Cush begat Nimrod: he began to be a mighty one in the earth. Vs 9 He was a mighty hunter before the LORD: wherefore it is said, Even as Nimrod the mighty hunter before the LORD.

He was written and depicts innovation and inventions of mankind.

Right from Moses' writings, there were laws to guide the individuals of the nation of Israel on what to do and how to do what was to be done. Beyond that, there were judges that were appointed too.

> **Deuteronomy 19:17** Then both the men, between whom the controversy is, shall stand before the LORD, before the priests and the judges, which shall be in those days;

> **Deuteronomy 19:19-20** Then shall ye do unto him, as he had thought to have done unto his brother, so shalt thou put the evil away from among you. Vs 20 And those which remain shall hear, and fear, and shall henceforth commit no more any such evil among you.

Clearly, the goal of witnesses and judges is fairness. The essence was to put away evil from the land (from amongst them).

> **Leviticus 19:17-18** Thou shalt not hate thy brother in thine heart: thou shalt in any wise rebuke thy neighbour, and not suffer sin upon him. Vs 18 Thou shalt not avenge, nor bear any grudge against the

children of thy people, but thou shalt love thy neighbour as thyself: I am the LORD.

This is the same with human government. Thus, human governments today can be seen as seeking to achieve fairness, orderliness and peaceful lifestyle and livelihood of the citizenry. In essence, the intent of governmental laws and statutes will be peace, fairness and orderliness which is within God's righteousness.

This explains what Paul taught in his letter to the Romans:

Romans 13:1-4 Let every soul be subject unto the higher powers. For there is no power but of God: the powers that be are ordained of God. Vs 2 Whosoever therefore resisteth the power, resisteth the ordinance of God: and they that resist shall receive to themselves damnation. Vs 3 For rulers are not a terror to good works, but to the evil. Wilt thou then not be afraid of the power? do that which is good, and thou shalt have praise of the same: Vs 4 For he is the minister of God to thee for good. But if thou do that which is evil, be afraid; for he beareth not the sword in vain: for he is the minister of God, a revenger to execute wrath upon him that doeth evil.

Now, observe the use of the term 'ordained by God'. The word 'ordained' was translated from the Greek word 'tasso' which means appointed. Paul here in an undertone, writes that God instructs orderliness. This is similar to how Paul wrote using the Adam and Eve narrative for husband

and wife by teaching that wives should be subject to their own husband

> **Ephesians 5:21-25** Submitting yourselves one to another in the fear of God. [22] Wives, submit yourselves unto your own husbands, as unto the Lord. [23] For the husband is the head of the wife, even as Christ is the head of the church: and he is the saviour of the body. [24] Therefore as the church is subject unto Christ, so let the wives be to their own husbands in every thing. [25] Husbands, love your wives, even as Christ also loved the church, and gave himself for it;

In Romans 13, Paul talks of orderliness in the society and he says God has ordained men to do so.

The word 'tasso' also occurs in:

> **Acts 13:48** And when the Gentiles heard this, they were glad, and glorified the word of the Lord: and as many as were ordained to eternal life believed.

> **Acts 15:2** When therefore Paul and Barnabas had no small dissension and disputation with them, they determined that Paul and Barnabas, and certain other of them, should go up to Jerusalem unto the apostles and elders about this question.

> **Acts 22:10** And I said, What shall I do, Lord? And the Lord said unto me, Arise, and go into Damascus; and

there it shall be told thee of all things which are appointed for thee to do.

Acts 28:22 But we desire to hear of thee what thou thinkest for as concerning this sect, we know that every where it is spoken against.

1 Corinthians 16:15 I beseech you, brethren, (ye know the house of Stephanas, that it is the firstfruits of Achaia, and that they have addicted themselves to the ministry of the saints,)

Back to Romans 13,

Paul writes that human governments are ordained of God and by so doing, he draws up a narrative that orderliness is of God and he tell us why.

Romans 13:2 Whosoever therefore resisteth the power, resisteth the ordinance of God: and they that resist shall receive to themselves damnation.

Here in verse 2, the word 'ordinance' is translated from the word 'diatage'. A word used for angels, and the law in:

Acts 7:53 Who have received the law by the disposition of angels, and have not kept it.

Romans 13:3 For rulers are not a terror to good works, but to the evil. Wilt thou then not be afraid of the power?

do that which is good, and thou shalt have praise of the same

Observe also, the term 'not a terror to good works' - that is, they are not supposed to scare anyone who does what is right.

The word 'praise' was translated from the Greek word 'epainos' which was written earlier in Romans 2:29.

> **Romans 2:29** But he is a Jew, which is one inwardly; and circumcision is that of the heart, in the spirit, and not in the letter; whose praise is not of men, but of God.

In other words, he meant this is the reason for authority, that is, to be able to stop terror in the society. In the way nature is crafted, orderliness can be seen.

> **Romans 13:4** For he is the minister of God to thee for good. But if thou do that which is evil, be afraid; for he beareth not the sword in vain: for he is the minister of God, a revenger to execute wrath upon him that doeth evil.

He is referring to believers. Paul here, subtly writes for legalism in the society and orderliness.

> **Romans 13:5** Wherefore ye must needs be subject, not only for wrath, but also for conscience sake.

Paul explains that Christians who disobey earthly ordinance do not do good for the gospel of Christ. This simply means that we have a responsibility to be responsible citizens as believers. In other words, Paul explains that some laid down rules and regulations by human governments are not persecution or oppositions to the gospel, rather, the essence is to achieve orderliness

Paul was exemplary before human government in his time in Acts 16 and Acts 21-23

At a point, he appealed to Caesar. He mentioned that he was a Roman citizen; freeborn. He gave proper respect to earthly laws and rules.

> **Romans 13:4-5** For he is the minister of God to thee for good. But if thou do that which is evil, be afraid; for he beareth not the sword in vain: for he is the minister of God, a revenger to execute wrath upon him that doeth evil. Vs 5 Wherefore ye must needs be subject, not only for wrath, but also for conscience sake.

Hence, Christians should not be law breakers in the society. Paul in his letter to Timothy explains how the government should be prayed for:

> **1 Timothy 2:1-4** I exhort therefore, that, first of all, supplications, prayers, intercessions, and giving of thanks, be made for all men; [2] For kings, and for all that are in authority; that we may lead a quiet and peaceable life in all godliness and honesty. [3] For this is

good and acceptable in the sight of God our Saviour; [4] Who will have all men to be saved, and to come unto the knowledge of the truth.

This means that those in human governments / authority are to be seen as those needing to receive salvation. In doing so, they walk properly in God's kingdom. The role of the church and support for the rule of law or societal order is a critical aspect to understand. The government of the state is responsible to ensure a peaceful and prosperous society, where lives, property and values of the society are duly and properly protected. The government policies and orders are supposed to be in the best interest of the safety of men; where it does not secure lives then it is tyrannical and not the ideal.

In every organisation, authority is bestowed because of responsibility and not just in a vacuum. Hence, the officers of the state and civil servants who enforce the law and restrictions of the state should not be stigmatized, but treated with honour.

Therefore, the apostles of the church of Christ teach to obey human authority and the rule of law. The admonition to be full of good works which includes obeying laws and regulations by the government was emphatically stressed.

- The use of Technology, media. social media, and their boundaries.

The Encyclopaedia Britannica defines the word "science" as any system of knowledge that is concerned with the physical world and its phenomena and that entails unbiased observations and systemic experimentation.

While "Technology" is the application of scientific knowledge to the practical aims of human life or as it is sometimes phrased, to the change and manipulation of the human environment.

The Merriam-Webster English Dictionary defines "science" as something that may be studied or learned like a systemized knowledge, and "Technology" is defined as the scientific method of achieving a practical purpose, in other words technology is the use/application of science in solving problems.

From these definitions above, science and technology can be said to involve the following:

1) Man (who): As the developer and controller of ideas, methods and products.

2) Knowledge, methods (how): where man seeks to find out via the cycle of continual research and application (experimentation) of his discovered methods.

3) What: It involves objects (devices, products) and recurrent adaptation/manipulation of these to meet emerging needs.

4) Why: In order for man to improve/take advantage of the physical world(environment) he lives in.

A lot of events have changed in history since the emergence of scientific innovations as man manipulates his environment to meet his "perceived" needs or to create value.

Note that this would result in the need to distinguish what man thinks he needs from what God says man needs, or what man sees/creates as value from what God places value on. The Bible alludes to scientific development and innovations in the earth:

Bible Allusion to Science and Technology

Food (cultivation, processing, occupation and its tools)

> **Genesis 2:5** And every plant of the field before it was in the earth, and every herb of the field before it grew: for the LORD God had not caused it to rain upon the earth, and there was not a man to till the ground.

The word "till" implies to be a husbandman, to cultivate, this alludes to man's means of providing food via crops of the earth.

> **Genesis 9:20** And Noah began to be an husbandman, and he planted a vineyard:

> **Genesis 26:12** Then Isaac sowed in that land, and received in the same year an hundredfold: and the LORD blessed him, Va 13 And the man waxed great, and went forward, and grew until he became very great: Vs 14 For he had possession of flocks, and possession of herds, and great store of servants: and the Philistines envied him.

Observe in the above verse that material possession/value became a source of envy amongst humans.

> **2nd Chronicles 26:10** Also he built towers in the desert, and digged many wells: for he had much cattle, both in the low country, and in the plains: husbandmen also, and vine dressers in the mountains, and in Carmel: for he loved husbandry.

Jesus in his parables referenced the use of fishing nets in the catch of sea creatures for food Matthew 13:47-50,

> **Matthew 13:47-50** Again, the kingdom of heaven is like unto a net, that was cast into the sea, and gathered of every kind: [48] Which, when it was full, they drew to shore, and sat down, and gathered the good into vessels,

> but cast the bad away. [49] So shall it be at the end of the world: the angels shall come forth, and sever the wicked from among the just, [50] And shall cast them into the furnace of fire: there shall be wailing and gnashing of teeth.

This also served as occupation for men, man's means of financial/material value, Matthew 4:18-22, Mark 1:16-20, Luke 5:1-11,

> **Matthew 4:18** And Jesus, walking by the sea of Galilee, saw two brethren, Simon called Peter, and Andrew his casting a net into the sea: for Vs 19 And he saith unto them, Follow me, and I will make you fishers of men. Vs 20 And they straightway left their nets, and followed him. Vs 21 And going from thence, he saw other two brethren, James the son of Zebedee, and John his brother, in a ship with Zebedee their father, mending their nets; and he called them. Vs 22 And they immediately left the ship and their father, and followed him.

Notice however that Jesus' discipleship places more value on lives, by making them fishers of men".

> **Luke 24:41** And while they yet believed not for joy, and wondered, he said unto them, Have ye here any meat? Vs 42 And they gave him a piece of a broiled fish, and of an honeycomb. Vs 43 And he took it, and did eat before them.

John 21:5 Then Jesus saith unto them, Children, have ye any meat? They answered him, No. Vs 6 And he said unto them, Cast the net on the right side of the ship, and ye shall find. They cast therefore, and now they were not able to draw it for the multitude of fishes. Vs 7 Therefore that disciple whom Jesus loved saith unto Peter, It is the Lord. Now when Simon Peter heard that it was the Lord, he girt his fisher's coat unto him, (for he was naked,) and did cast himself into the sea. Vs 8 And the other disciples came in a little ship; (for they were not far from land, but as it were two hundred cubits,) dragging the net with fishes. Vs 9 As soon then as they were come to land, they saw a fire of coals there, and fish laid thereon, and bread. Vs 10 Jesus saith unto them, Bring of the fish which ye have now caught. Vs 11 Simon Peter went up, and drew the net to land full of great fishes, an hundred and fifty and three: and for all there were so many, yet was not the net broken. Vs 12 Jesus saith unto them, Come and dine. And none of the disciples durst ask him, who art thou? knowing that it was the Lord. Vs 13 Jesus then cometh, and taketh bread, and giveth them, and fish likewise.

Man explored his world scientifically to develop methods for food harvesting on land, in water, food processing via heat (bread, fish), and today there are improved farming and food processing systems making more food available with lesser effort.

Construction (buildings, wells, metal work, weaponry, stones)

> **Genesis 4:17** And Cain knew his wife; and she conceived, and bare Enoch: and he builded a city, and called the name of the city, after the name of his son, Enoch.

The word 'Cain' is derived from the Hebrew word 'quayin' derived from another word 'qunah' which means possession or weaponry. Cain built a city, he is also the forefather of those who established tools, the harp, organ, brass works, iron, weaponry which is the foundation of urbanization.

> **Genesis 4:21** And his brother's name was Jubal: he was the father of all such as handle the harp and organ. Vs 22 And Zillah, she also bare Tubalcain, an instructer of every artificer in brass and iron: and the sister of Tubalcain as Naamah. Vs23 And Lamech said unto his wives, Adah and Zillah, Hear my voice; ye wives of Lamech, hearken unto my speech: for I have slain a man to my wounding and a young man to my hurt.

The word 'artificer' was translated from the Hebrew word 'choresh'. It is a word used for a fabricator; inventor of machines, while the word brass means something made of metal. This can be traced to the beginning of all human development/innovation.

Paul in Ephesians 6:10-19 used the imagery of the armour costume of the Roman band of soldiers: the helmet. breastplate, sword, shield.

Noah built an ark, a large boat to preserve lives from the flood.

> **Genesis 6:14** Make thee an ark of gopher wood; rooms shalt thou make in the ark, and shalt pitch it within and without with pitch. Vs 15 And this is the fashion which thou shalt make it of: The length of the ark shall be three hundred cubits, the breadth of it fifty cubits, and the height of it thirty cubits. Vs 16 A window shalt thou make to the ark, and in a cubit shalt thou finish it above; and the door of the ark shalt thou set in the side thereof; with lower, second, and third stories shalt thou make it

The building of the tower of Babel in Genesis 11. Men built cities, walls, gates, developed bands of soldiers.

> **2nd Chronicles 26:6** And he went forth and warred against the Philistines, and brake down the wall of Gath, and the wall of Jabneh, and the wall of Ashdod, and built cities about Ashdod, and among the Philistines....Vs 9 Moreover Uzziah built towers in Jerusalem at the corner gate, and at the valley gate and at the turning of the wall, and fortified them. Vs 10 Also he built towers in the desert, and digged many wells: for he had much cattle, both in the low country, and in the plains: husbandmen also, and vine dressers in the mountains, and in Carmel: for he loved husbandry. Vs

11 Moreover Uzziah and host of fighting men, that went out to war by bajetel according to the number of their account by the hand of Jeiel the scribe and Maaseiah the ruler, under the hand of Hananiah, one of the king's captains.

Psalm 20:7 mentions chariots, horses as used in wars. Isaiah spoke about those who beat their swords into plowshares and their spears into pruning hooks

Isaiah 2:4 And he shall judge among the nations, and shall rebuke many people: and they shall beat their swords into plowshares, and their spears into pruninghooks: nation shall not lift up sword against nation, neither shall they learn war any more. Vs 5 O house of Jacob, come ye, and let us walk in the light of the LORD. Vs 6 Therefore thou hast forsaken thy people the house of Jacob, because they be replenished from the east, and are soothsayers like the Philistines, and they please themselves in the children of strangers. Vs 7 Their land also is full of silver and gold, neither is there any end of their treasures; their land is also full of horses, neither is there any end of their chariots: Vs 8 Their land also is full of idols; they worship the work of their own hands, that which their own fingers have made.

Observe also that alongside their innovations, was the development of human means of governance, the ambition and strive for supremacy/dominance over men. This was achieved by the invention of weaponry.

> **Acts 23:20** And he said, The Jews have agreed to desire thee that thou wouldest bring down Paul tomorrow into the council, as though they would enquire somewhat of him more perfectly. Vs 21 But do not thou yield unto them: for there lie in wait for him of them more than forty men, which have bound themselves with an oath, that they will neither eat nor drink till they have killed him: and now are they ready, looking for a promise from thee. Vs 22 So the chief captain then let the young man depart, and charged him, See thou tell no man that thou hast shewed these things to me.

Communication/transmission of information:

Verbal (oral) communication from person to person, which sometimes could involve going some distance to ensure this is done. It is a form of human communication wherein knowledge, information, ideas or cultural materials are transmitted, received by word of mouth (speech) from one person to another. Oral tradition also made it possible to pass/preserve knowledge across generations before the advent of writing.

Then the written communication which could involve words, pictures, etc. An example is Moses who was the first to document historical facts of scripture which he got from the oral tradition and pictorial language of the Jews.

Having learned in Egypt, he put down these facts in a written format, he employed Egyptian alphabets, stories and imageries to document the historical narratives of the Jews.

> **Deuteronomy 31:9** And Moses wrote this law, and delivered it unto the priests the sons of Levi, which bare the ark of the covenant of the LORD, and unto all the elders of Israel.

The word "wrote" was translated from the Hebrew word "kathab". It means to write, to inscribe, describe or record. It appears 223 times in the Old Testament books of the Bible. The statement "Moses wrote" proves his education; literacy and skill in writing.

> **2 Timothy 3:16** All scripture is given by inspiration of Ged. and is profitable for doctrine, for reproof, for correction, for instruction in righteousness:

God inspired men to document scripture in order to teach, convince men concerning salvation, and produce spiritual growth.

> **2nd Timothy 4:13** The cloke that I left at Troas with Carpus, when thou comest, bring with thee, and the books, but especially the parchments.

Before the advent of the printing press, the preservation of and access to scripture in history was via the science of writing, these materials were copied and distributed.

Also, information systems have been made more efficient with the development of mobile devices providing faster access, transmission and preservation of information from any part of the world.

Power generation and transportation of persons and goods

The advent of sophisticated engines developed from the history of power generation via heat, water, natural fuels, to advanced sophisticated automobile systems which enhance swift transportation from one place to the other as against man's efforts via barefoot transportation, domesticating animals, chariots. Via science and innovation, man also explored transportation via floating on water,

> **1st Kings 5:9** My servants shall bring them down from Lebanon unto the sea: and I will convey them by sea in floats unto the place that thou shalt appoint me, and will cause them to be discharged there, and thou shalt receive them: and thou shalt accomplish my desire, in giving food for my household.

> **2nd Chronicles 2:16** And we will cut wood out of Lebanon, as much as thou shalt need: and we will bring it to thee in floats by sea to Joppa; and thou shalt carry it up to Jerusalem.

> **Jonah 1:3** Jonah transported himself via ship

Jesus used boats as means of transportation in his ministry Luke 5:3, John 6:22-23,

> **Acts 27:30** And as the shipmen were about to flee out of the ship when they had let down the boat into the sea, under foreship, Vs 31 Paul said to the centurion and to the soldiers, the soldiers cut off the ropes of the boat, and let her fall off

Today the development of transport means by air has facilitated quicker access to and across continents.

Technological advancement in health and medicine

With the aim of medicine being to promote and maintain health and wellbeing, medical science has advanced proactive and reactive approach to health. From the scriptural history of the washings in the Jewish laws, which can be said to be a practice of hygiene in medicine

> **Leviticus 15:1-13** And the Lord spake unto Moses and to Aaron, saying, [2] Speak unto the children of Israel, and say unto them, When any man hath a running issue out of his flesh, because of his issue he is unclean. [3] And this shall be his uncleanness in his issue: whether his flesh run with his issue, or his flesh be stopped from

his issue, it is his uncleanness. [4] Every bed, whereon he lieth that hath the issue, is unclean: and every thing, whereon he sitteth, shall be unclean. [5] And whosoever toucheth his bed shall wash his clothes, and bathe himself in water, and be unclean until the even. [6] And he that sitteth on any thing whereon he sat that hath the issue shall wash his clothes, and bathe himself in water, and be unclean until the even. [7] And he that toucheth the flesh of him that hath the issue shall wash his clothes, and bathe himself in water, and be unclean until the even. [8] And if he that hath the issue spit upon him that is clean; then he shall wash his clothes, and bathe himself in water, and be unclean until the even. [9] And what saddle soever he rideth upon that hath the issue shall be unclean. [10] And whosoever toucheth any thing that was under him shall be unclean until the even: and he that beareth any of those things shall wash his clothes, and bathe himself in water, and be unclean until the even. [11] And whomsoever he toucheth that hath the issue, and hath not rinsed his hands in water, he shall wash his clothes, and bathe himself in water, and be unclean until the even. [12] And the vessel of earth, that he toucheth which hath the issue, shall be broken: and every vessel of wood shall be rinsed in water. [13] And when he that hath an issue is cleansed of his issue; then he shall number to himself seven days for his cleansing, and wash his clothes, and bathe his flesh in running water, and shall be clean.

Observe that sanitising and hygiene principles were observed and contaminated garments were to be washed. Today, scientific methods are advanced and enhance health maintenance.

Furthermore, technological advancement in media has gone to greater heights today such that we now have various forms of media. Over time, the forms of media that are primarily in use have changed.

Media can be broadly or generally classified into three types - print, broadcast, and internet. While print media (which includes newspapers, magazines, books, banners, billboards etc) is the oldest form of media, in current times, internet media is the most relevant (which includes social media, podcasts, forums).

The media as a whole has been very useful in truly making the world a global village such that with just a mobile device one can access information from virtually any part of the World.

Social media platforms (such as Facebook, Twitter, Instagram etc.) have audiences into billions in virtually every nation.

For the gospel there has been no better time in history to make the message of Christ and Him crucified more available, even the hitherto "Anti-Christian" territories will have to contend with the almost unarrestable influence of technology.

However, coming with this ease of information and communication is the flip side to everything. With the same ease one need not go around like Paul will say to be a "busy body", to gossip, all I in need is a phone, evil communication isn't as long drawn, with WhatsApp, Facebook messenger etc I can chat with "satan" himself with no form of interference or observation by anyone. I can do more without being seen and sin as much too.

Also, I can lie, fabricate stories, add to people's words or take away and before I retract or it's refuted or rebutted, a billion people would have believed and acted on it and the truth might never be known. A phone will further make the Solomonic wisdom of guarding my mind rather more demanding as adult content sites need not be browsed, they stare at one on Facebook/the Internet, available with ease of Chat messaging, also adultery and fornication require no more than the discretion of locking one's device and arranging for covert and sinister modus operandi to engage in illicit affairs .

Furthermore, coming with all these is the spirit of the world is lightness, looseness, loquaciousness. The freedom to be "free, say anything, address anyone without recourse to respect and regard" - they say "after all it affords the garb of anonymity". Godlessness, that is, the ungodly have found stronger voices to attack the scriptures. They do it with ease and need not gather people to do so. Just post it and it reaches millions of minds.

Churches and ministries today can hardly maintain their sanctity of both information and oversight of the same without the media making it impossible for "David not to tell it in Gath nor declare not on the streets of Ashkelon" as the messenger needs just tweet it for all "Ashkelonites "and "Gathites "to have the Information. Twisted, bent, fabricated, dishonouring, it doesn't matter, just tell it and rebroadcast it, the world has moved since the psalmist.

Therefore, without much ado, the believer Must do the Word without adapting himself to the world but rather subject the World to the Word.

He must take Paul's warnings seriously

> **Ephesians 5:15-16** See then that ye walk circumspectly, not as fools, but as wise, Vs 16 Redeeming the time, because the days are evil.

This age (times) is evil and Satan is its god. He mustn't forget Paul's forewarning too:

> **2 Timothy 4:3-4** For the time will come when they will not endure sound doctrine; but after their own lusts shall they heap to themselves teachers, having itching ears. Vs 4 And they shall turn away their ears from the truth, and shall be turned unto fables.

He must remember the words Jesus told the 12:

Matthew 10:16 Behold, I send you forth as sheep in the midst of wolves: be ye therefore wise as serpents, and harmless as doves.

Very needful now.

We must use every media to teach the gospel and reach the unreached. We must however not allow the media, its spirit and Broadways to review the scriptures and be so maltreated that certain emerging attitudes from the social media relegates Christian principles to the background. If we refuse and follow the world, the inherent repercussions are innumerable and we can't afford it.

As believer, as we Facebook, tweet, blog and surf the net we must remember to:

Proverbs 4:23 Keep thy heart with all diligence; for out of it are the issues of life.

And when I read or glance unedifying comments or articles, I must never forget

Romans 12:2 And be not conformed to this world: but be ye transformed by the renewing of your mind, that ye may prove what is that good, and acceptable, and perfect, will of God.

Finally, never forgetting that the Church I should belong to, be submitted to and be pastored through is NOT my friends list on Facebook or Twitter or blackberry. Different times, changing seasons, subtle devils but the never changing word in an ever-changing world remains my anchor through these storms. In all, the local church must uphold its identity, purpose and function in the world, yesterday, today and always, as God's beacon of light in a dark world and never yield to or adapt to the systems and practices of this world.

CONCLUSION

The believer and the church must see themselves as washed, sanctified and separate from this world.

> **1 Corinthians 6:9** Know ye not that the unrighteous shall not inherit the kingdom of God? Be not deceived: neither fornicators, nor idolaters, nor adulterers, nor effeminate, nor abusers of themselves with mankind,

The word 'kingdom' was translated from the Greek word 'basileia'. It can include judgement, deciding matters, etc. The word inherit' means to be part of something. it was translated from the Greek word 'kleronomeo'.

> **1 Corinthians 6:10-11** Nor thieves, nor covetous, nor drunkards, nor revilers, nor extortioners, shall inherit the kingdom of God. Vs 11 And such were some of you: but ye are washed, but ye are sanctified, but ye are justified in the name of the Lord Jesus, and by the Spirit of our God.

We have been washed, sanctified and justified in Christ Jesus. Christ keeps his church holy, so, must we walk in the fact that we are separate from this world.

Paul writes to the church in Corinth and tells them not to handle matters like this world. They had seen brothers take matters in a worldly manner by going to the courts. He lets them know that conduct is not of the body of Christ.

Believers must be careful about allowing the ideas, nuances and communication of this world get into them. The local church and its leadership should be much more careful. Paul in the letter to the Romans instructs that they renew their minds.

> **Romans 12:1-2** I beseech you therefore, brethren, by the mercies of God, that ye present your bodies a living sacrifice, holy, acceptable unto God, which is your reasonable service. Vs 2 And be not conformed to this world: but be ye transformed by the renewing of your mind, that ye may prove what is that good, and acceptable, and perfect, will of God.

believers and the church should see themselves as service unto the Lord and therefore must be careful about their conduct, what they do, what they see, where they visit and friends they make. Paul warned about evil communication.

1st Corinthians 15:33 Be not deceived: evil communications corrupt good manners.

The fact that technology is bringing in new advancements does not mean the believer should adopt them and allow them to change the very intricate details of our faith. The scriptures remain our guide, belief, rule book for our practices and not the norm of the day.

We must know that we are in this world and we are not of this world.

> **John 17:16** They are not of the world, even as I am not of the world.

The local church therefore should stick with the traditions of the church as it is in the scriptures and not try to modify or amend it into the mould of the modern-day world. Christianity has its core values and traditions that does not change with time. The believer on the other hand should seek to serve the Lord with all his heart and soul and must not seek to do this outside the assembly of believers, for that is where he receives guidance, nurturing, correction and growth.

Made in the USA
Columbia, SC
30 June 2024

37927666R00134